the
attention
fix

ALSO BY ANDERS HANSEN

The ADHD Advantage

The Mind-Body Method

The Happiness Cure

the attention fix

How to Focus
in a World That
Wants to
Distract You

Dr. Anders Hansen

Zeitgeist • New York

Published in the United States by Zeitgeist™, an imprint and division of Penguin Random House LLC, New York.
zeitgeistpublishing.com

Zeitgeist™ is a trademark of Penguin Random House LLC

Originally published in Swedish as *Skärmhjärnan* in 2019 by Bonnier Fakta, Stockholm, Sweden. Copyright © 2019 by Anders Hansen.
This translation published in the United Kingdom by Vermilion, an imprint of Ebury Publishing, a division of Penguin Random House Ltd., London in 2023.
Ebury is part of the Penguin Random House group of companies.

Published by arrangement with Salomonsson Agency

ISBN: 9780593885833
Ebook ISBN: 9780593886199

Printed in the United States of America
1st Printing

First US Edition

Dedicated to

Hans-Åke Hansen (1940–2011),
Vanja Hansen, Björn Hansen

The most important relic of early humans is the modern mind.

STEVEN PINKER

CONTENTS

PREFACE

IN MAY OF 2018, I attended the American Psychiatric Association's (APA) annual meeting in New York, where 10,000 colleagues from around the world gather in one place—nowhere is the word "bipolar" mentioned more often—to hear from world-leading brain scientists about their latest findings.

When attending conferences like the APA's, it's not always what's being said in the lectures that is the most interesting part. At least as exciting is getting a sense of the issues that interest and concern psychiatrists and researchers the most. In the spring of 2018, I heard many colleagues ask each other the same recurring question: "What are we really exposing ourselves to with digitalization? Are we in fact conducting a gigantic experiment with ourselves and our children as guinea pigs?"

No one had a definitive answer, but everyone agreed that the changes we have seen in human behavior over the last ten years—in terms of how we communicate with and compare ourselves to each other—are extremely far-reaching and might affect us on a deeper level than we think. Many suspected that the vast increase in the number of young people in particular seeking help for mental health problems over the past decade may be at least partly due to our swift embracing of a digital lifestyle.

Even though my colleagues seemed to have more questions than answers, we are not entirely clueless. Research into the effects of digitalization on the brain may be in its infancy, but our knowledge is growing by the day.

After the APA conference, I realized that never in human history have we changed our behavior as rapidly as we have in the last few decades. And it's not just our digital habits that have changed. We are also experiencing a different form of stress than in the past, while also sleeping less and being more sedentary. All of this means that the brain has ventured into uncharted territory. This book is about the consequences.

Anders Hansen

CHAPTER 1

THE WORLD THAT SHAPED US

. . . .
. . . .
. . . .
. . . .
. . . .
. . . .
. . . .
. . . .
. . . .
. . . .
. . . .
. . . .
. . . .
. . . .
. . . .
. . . .
. . . .
. . . .
. . . .
. . . .
. . . .
. . . .
. . . .
. . . .
. . . .
. . . .
. . . .
. . . .

. . . .
. . . .
. . . .
. . . .
. . . .
. . . .
. . . .
. . . .
. . . .
. . . .
. . . .
. . . .
. . . .
. . . .

The pages you have just flipped through contain 10,000 dots. Imagine that each dot corresponds to one generation of humans since our species emerged in East Africa some 200,000 years ago. All the dots combined represent the history of humanity. How many of these generations lived in the world you and I know—with cars, electricity, running water and TV sets?

. . . . (8 dots)

How many lived in a world with computers, cell phones and air travel?

. . . (3)

How many have never experienced anything but a world with smartphones, Facebook and the internet?

. (1)

This book is about the most advanced structure we know of in the universe, the seat of everything we have experienced—our feelings, memories and consciousness: our brain. This is an organ that in a strange way feels both alien and a little frightening to us, but at the same time *is* us. The brain has been molded over eons of time to fit the world in which it exists—a world radically different from the one you and I, who make up the last few dots, are familiar with.

Evolution—the basis of life on earth

You and I are the result of a process without meaning or purpose. Evolution is neither good nor evil, benevolent nor malevolent. It's an essential condition for life on earth and the process through which we adapt to the world around us. But how does it work when evolution adapts all species to their environment? As an example, let's consider a group of bears in North America, venturing farther and farther north until they eventually reach Alaska, where they wander about in the Arctic cold. The bears' brown fur makes it difficult for them to camouflage themselves against the snow, so they are often spotted by the seals that are the only prey around. The bears get to the brink of starvation.

In one of the female bear's egg cells, a random change—known as a mutation—occurs in a gene that affects the color of the bear's fur, making it white. The cub born with white fur has an easier time sneaking up on seals than the other bears. This makes it better at hunting, which in turn increases its chances of surviving and eventually having cubs of its own. These are also born with white fur and are therefore more likely to survive and have their own cubs. And so on. Gradually, the brown bears are outcompeted, and after a time—which might be tens or hundreds of thousands of years—many bears in Alaska have white fur. So white that we call them polar bears.

Any hereditary trait that increases an organism's chances of survival and reproduction will become increasingly common over time. In this way, all plants and animals—including humans—have adapted to their environment. If gradually spreading the white fur color through a population of bears sounds like evolutionary grunt work, that's exactly what it is. It takes a long time—a *really* long time—for major changes to occur within a species.

Instead of a polar bear, now let's imagine a human living on the savannah, say 100,000 years ago—we'll call her Anna. Anna finds a tree full of sweet, high-calorie fruits; she eats a fruit and walks away feeling satisfied and content. The next morning, she is hungry again and decides to go back for more, but by then the fruit is gone; someone else has picked it. In the world Anna inhabits, the empty tree can be a matter of life and death, as 15–20 percent of all people die of starvation.

Now let's imagine another woman, Mary, living on the same savannah. Mary carries a mutation in a gene that affects how she experiences the taste of sugar. When she bites into one of the sweet fruits, her brain releases a particularly large amount of a molecule called dopamine, which plays a role in making us feel good and motivating us to do various things (you can read more about dopamine on page 38).

As a result, she gets a violent urge to eat *all* the fruit on the tree. She doesn't settle for just one but gobbles up as many as she can. After a while, she is full and stumbles off. The next morning, Mary wakes up and wants something sweet again. But when she returns to the tree, someone has already picked the handful of fruits she left behind. Bad news, yes, but she ate so many the day before that she has built up a reserve.

It's not hard to guess that Mary is the woman with the best chance of survival. The calories she doesn't use are stored in her body as abdominal fat, protecting her from starvation when times are tough. This means that Mary has a better chance of passing on her genes by having children. And because her calorie cravings are caused by a gene (although, in reality, a number of genes rather than a single gene contribute to cravings), the same trait is passed on to the next generation, who in turn will have a better chance of surviving and procreating. Gradually, more and more children are born with a strong craving for calories, and they all have a better chance of making it. Slowly but surely, over thousands of years, the craving for calories becomes an increasingly common trait among the population.

But let's transplant Anna and Mary into the modern world of fast-food restaurants. When Anna spots a McDonald's, she goes inside for a burger, leaving satisfied and not too full. When Mary walks into the McDonald's, however, she orders a burger with fries, Coca-Cola and ice cream, leaving the restaurant absolutely stuffed. The next morning, she wakes up hungry again and returns to find the restaurant as fully stocked as the day before. She orders the same meal as yesterday.

After a few months, this gluttony has taken a toll on Mary's body. Not only has she put on quite a few excess pounds, she has also begun to develop type 2 diabetes as her body is struggling to cope with her soaring blood sugar. Now, the roles are reversed. The hunger for calories that enabled Mary to survive on the savannah isn't an asset in today's world. Suddenly the same biological mechanism that helped us survive for 99.9 percent of our time on earth is doing more harm than good.

This is not some hypothetical example but exactly what has happened. We have brought the calorie craving that evolution built into us over millions of years into the modern world, where calories are practically free. And the transition has taken place in the span of just a few generations—such a short time that we haven't had a chance to adapt. Biologically, we still have brains that react to each calorie by crying out: *Put that in your mouth, tomorrow there might be none left!*

We are constantly preparing ourselves for a famine that never comes and the result of this is clear to see: rates of obesity and type 2 diabetes are exploding worldwide. While we don't know exactly what our ancestors weighed, we can get a hint by looking at African tribes still living in pre-industrial societies who have an average body mass index (BMI) of around 20 (at the lower end of normal weight). In the US today, the average BMI is 28.8 and in Sweden it's 25.8.

The problems of excess weight and obesity are particularly pronounced in countries that have made the leap from poverty to lower-middle income in just a few decades. These countries have gone from living under a constant threat of famine to the Western fast-food culture in a generation.

It's not just our physical traits that may be out of sync with the modern world; the same is true of our mental ones. Let's say that Mary was constantly worrying about dangers, devising careful plans for how to avoid them. In a time when lots of people died in accidents, were beaten to death by other humans or were eaten by animals, this probably improved her chances of survival. But as Mary moves through life in the much safer world of today, this constant catastrophizing makes her feel unwell, giving her anxiety and phobias.

Constantly scanning their surroundings and being hyperactive and easily distracted allowed earlier humans to quickly seize opportunities and avoid danger. That rustling in the bush might be something edible, so best go check! Today, the same impulsive behavior and sensitivity to sensory stimuli make it difficult for children to concentrate and sit still in the classroom—leading them to be diagnosed with attention-deficit/hyperactivity disorder (ADHD).

We are not adapted to today's world

Since humans, like other animals, have evolved in response to the world around us, I think we can better understand ourselves by looking at the world that elicited our characteristics. An overwhelming majority of all generations of humans—9,500 out of the 10,000 dots—lived as hunter-gatherers. Their world was vastly different from the one you and I inhabit, though it's hard to say exactly what it looked like. We only know roughly how they lived, as nothing has been recorded from this prehistoric time. Moreover, we shouldn't generalize too much, as the living conditions of different groups of hunter-gatherers probably differed at least as much as ours do across the world today. Yet despite our limited knowledge and difficulties generalizing, we can still summarize a number of overall differences between their world and ours:

Back then, people lived in groups of 50–150 individuals. Today, the majority of the world's population lives in cities.

Back then, people were constantly on the move and had simple settlements. Today, we live in the same place for years or even decades.

Back then, in your whole life you might see a few hundred, or at most a few thousand, individuals, who looked much like you. Today, we see millions of people from all over the world in a lifetime.

Back then, half of all people died before their tenth birthday. Today, only a few percent die before the age of ten.

Back then, the average life expectancy was barely 30 years. Today, life expectancy in the US is 80 for women and 75 for men.

Back then, the most common causes of death were starvation, dehydration, infection, bleeding out and being bludgeoned to death. Today, the top causes of death are cardiovascular disease and cancer.

Back then, 10–15 percent of people were killed by another person. Today, less than 1 percent of all deaths are due to murder, war or civil war—i.e., caused by another human being.

Back then, in order to survive you had to be easily distracted and constantly scanning your surroundings for danger. Today, we consider the ability *not* to be distracted as one of the most important human qualities. The same dangers no longer exist.

Back then, anyone who wasn't on the move trying to find something to eat risked starving to death. Today, we don't have to take a single step to find food—it can easily be ordered right to our doorstep.

So, in a whole range of ways, we have made huge changes to our environment in just a couple of millennia—or even a couple of centuries! "A couple of millennia" sounds like an eternity to you and me, but in evolutionary terms it's a flash in the pan. As a result, we have evolved for a completely different world and find ourselves out of sync with the times we live in. To understand the consequences, let's start by taking a closer look at the organ from which all our thoughts, feelings and experiences arise: the human brain.

Feelings are survival strategies

From your first breath to your very last, your brain is trying to answer one single question: *What should I do now?* The brain doesn't care what happened yesterday; it's focused entirely on the present and the future. To assess the situation you are in, it uses memories and tries to nudge you in the right direction with the help of feelings. But its goal is not to make you feel good, climb the corporate ladder or stay healthy—it's to do the things that helped your ancestors survive and pass on their genes.

Feelings are not reactions to the world around us but something our

brains create as a reaction to what's happening inside our bodies, combined with what's happening around us.

The purpose is to guide us toward different behaviors. Does that sound strange? Let's take it from the beginning. We want to understand and control our feelings, especially when we aren't feeling good, but to do so we need to understand what feelings really are and why we have them, because feelings play a much more important function than simply giving you and me a rich inner life.

Like in any other species, evolution has shaped the human body and brain around one basic principle: survive and pass on your genes. Evolution has tried a number of different strategies for achieving this, such as allowing some species to be so fast that they can outrun their enemies, or to camouflage themselves to avoid discovery. Another strategy is to have traits that allow you to access food others can't, like the giraffe, whose long neck allows it to eat leaves that are out of reach for other animals. Yet another strategy is to ensure that the species in question—in this case, humans—behaves in a way that allows it to survive. Feelings are essentially survival strategies, just like the giraffe's long neck or the polar bear's white fur. But instead of a physical attribute, feelings are a mechanism that helps us act swiftly, flexibly and forcefully.

Feelings guide us toward different decisions

All human activity—from scratching your chin to detonating an atomic bomb—is the result of one single thing: a desire to change your inner mental state. This is the starting point for how feelings guide us. When we are threatened, we feel scared or angry and, as a consequence, we either flee or attack. When our bodies are low on energy, we feel hungry and search for food.

In a perfect world, we would have all the information we need to make the choices we face. Someone thinking of eating a sandwich would know exactly what nutrients it contains, how it tastes and whether the bread is freshly baked. They would also know whether their body's nutrient stores are in need of replenishment and whether a sandwich is the best way to refill them. This would allow them to weigh up all the information and make a rational decision about whether or not to eat the sandwich. If one of our foremothers lived in such a "perfect world" and stood face-to-face with a beehive, she would have access to all the information about the risks and opportunities associated with the honey: how much honey and calories the beehive contains; what her energy stores look like; how likely she is to be stung if she empties the hive of its honey; whether there are other threats than just bees. Our foremother could then easily combine all the information and make a rational decision to either retrieve the honey or leave it be. The only problem is her world didn't look like that—and neither does ours.

This is where our feelings come into play by nudging us toward different behaviors and helping us act immediately and forcefully. When your conscious self doesn't have enough information or takes too long to decide, your brain does a quick calculation and delivers the answer in the form of a feeling: you feel overwhelming hunger and proceed to eat the sandwich. Similarly, your foremother would have felt hungry and decided to retrieve the honey if the risk of injury was low or if she was in desperate need of food. If the risk was too great, she would have felt fear and chosen to refrain.

When I stand in front of the pick 'n' mix in my local shop, the evolutionary algorithm developed to avoid starvation does a quick calculation and gives me the answer in the form of a violent craving for something sweet. Because our brains haven't had time to adapt to today's abundance of food, many of us struggle to make a rational decision when standing in the candy aisle. After all, we are much more likely to be the descendants of Mary and her calorie craving than Anna, who risked dying of starvation.

Negative feelings take top priority

So, for better or worse, feelings guide us toward different decisions. But they don't exist in a vacuum. Feelings are accompanied by a series of reactions in the body and in the brain that affect not only how our organs function, but also our mental processes and how we perceive the world around us.

When we feel scared, the brain quickly releases cortisol and adrenaline to make our heart beat faster and harder in order to pump more blood to the muscles in our body so that we can perform at our best—that is, flee or attack. If we see food when we are hungry, the brain releases dopamine to make us feel an urge to eat. Dopamine is also released when we feel sexually aroused. So is oxytocin, which creates a feeling of bonding between people, directing us to focus on the person sitting next to us and not on what's on TV.

Negative feelings take priority over positive ones, because historically they have often been linked to threats—which must be dealt with immediately. We can postpone eating, drinking, sleeping or mating until later, but we can't postpone acting in the face of a threat. That's why, under intense stress and anxiety, it's hard to think about anything else. Most likely, our ancestors experienced far more threats than opportunities in their environment. And if negative feelings were more common, that may explain why in most languages there are more words for negative feelings than for positive ones. What's more, most people find negative feelings more interesting. After all, who wants to watch a film or read a book without conflict or drama?

One major source of negative feelings is stress. In the next chapter, we will take a closer look at what stress really is.

CHAPTER 2

STRESS, ANXIETY AND DEPRESSION— EVOLUTIONARY WINNERS?

For 99 percent of the time of beasts on this planet, stress has been three minutes of terror after which it's either over with you or with your opponent. And what do we do? We turn on the same stress response for 30-year mortgages.

ROBERT SAPOLSKY, PROFESSOR OF BIOLOGY AND NEUROLOGY & NEUROLOGICAL SCIENCE AT STANFORD UNIVERSITY

FOR YOU AND ME, stress means not having your life together, failing to study for an exam or missing a deadline at work. From a historical perspective, these are not common ways of activating the brain's stress system.

Let's take a closer look at the system known in medical terms as the HPA axis, which is the result of millions of years of evolution and is found not only in humans but in virtually all vertebrates—such as birds, lizards, dogs, cats and apes. The HPA axis starts in a part of the brain called the hypothalamus (H). It sends a signal to the pituitary gland (P) at the base of the brain, which in turn asks the adrenal glands (A) on top of the kidneys to release a hormone called cortisol. Cortisol is the body's main stress hormone.

Presumably the HPA axis developed to help humans and animals respond to threats that were largely imminent. If one of your ancestors suddenly spotted a lion, the HPA axis would sound the alarm and signal to beware, mobilizing energy and making the heart beat faster and harder.

We have all felt our heart rate spike when we are stressed. But why does it do this? Well, in the situation with the lion, your ancestor had to act quickly and either attack or run away—*fight or flight*. In order to fight or to run as fast as possible, the body's muscles need more blood, and so the heart beats faster and harder. To this day, this mechanism lives on inside us and it is the reason why our pulse rises when we are stressed.

How the stress system evolved

The body's stress system—the HPA axis—exists for precisely the same reason that we have feelings: to help us survive. And like the rest of our body and brain, the stress system evolved to help our ancestors survive in their world, which was far more dangerous than ours. The dangers they faced were probably not only more frequent but also required immediate action. Most likely anyone who stood around for too long pondering whether to attack or run away from a lion was quickly removed from the gene pool.

Thankfully, nowadays most people rarely have to worry about life-threatening situations. Yet the same system in the brain is activated when we get stressed by psychosocial factors, like a deadline at work, a costly mortgage or not getting enough likes on social media. The stress we put on the HPA axis today is not as intense as when our ancestors were facing a lion, of course, but it can often last a long time—sometimes months or years. And the HPA axis probably wasn't designed for that. Exposing the brain to elevated levels of stress hormones over an extended period of time can cause it to stop functioning properly. This means constantly walking around in fight-or-flight mode, which leads the brain to deprioritize everything except fighting or fleeing. This is the brain's logic:

- Sleep—I'll do it later.
- Digesting food—I'll do it later.
- Procreating—I'll do it later.

Does this sound like you during stressful periods in life? Perhaps you have suffered from an upset stomach and nausea, as well as trouble sleeping and a reduced sex drive? Unfortunately, too many people share this experience. But the effects of prolonged stress are not at all strange once we realize that the brain is deprioritizing everything that doesn't involve immediate problem-solving. And the list of consequences of long-term stress doesn't end there because stress also affects our mental functions.

At the right dose, it sharpens our senses. But when stress becomes overwhelming, we can no longer think clearly.

Under severe stress, we don't use the most advanced and uniquely human part of our brain. Instead we regress to evolutionarily old and primitive parts. We tend to act quickly and forcefully, without using the "thinking" part of our brain. This can cause problems.

When we are under a lot of stress, we need either to fight or to flee and there is no room for subtlety. The brain wants you to make a quick decision and thus goes into troubleshooting mode, where immediate problem-solving—not social finesse—is priority number one. It reacts forcefully to the problems it detects in your surroundings, and as a result you might feel strong irritation over seemingly little things. *What the hell are the socks doing on the floor?*

We don't have time to be pleasant to those around us when we are under a lot of stress, which is why many of us develop a short fuse. Feelings of well-being allow us to let our guard down. But this is at the very bottom of the list of priorities for a brain under threat, which is why we often feel unwell during periods of severe stress. Another function the brain deprioritizes is storing long-term memories. Processing memories involves making connections between different areas of the brain. Responsible for this task is the hippocampus, the brain's memory center. In order for the connections—and thus the memory—to be strong, the hippocampus needs to run a signal through the newly formed memory circuits. But it can't do so under heavy stress. As a result, during stressful periods many people have poorer memory.

The amygdala—our smoke detector

On a summer's day in 2018, I was out hiking in the Italian Alps, when suddenly I stopped dead in my tracks in the middle of a steep, grassy meadow without knowing why. Even less did I know why my heart was suddenly beating hard and fast. My friend, walking a few steps behind me, asked if everything was OK. That's when I realized what had happened. Lying in the grass in front of me was a gray plastic tube that, from a few feet away, could have been mistaken for a snake. Without me being aware of it, my brain had been scanning my surroundings and when it detected the "snake," it sounded the alarm, causing me to stop. It took me a few seconds to realize it was only a plastic tube.

Today we understand the anatomy behind my reaction. The key player in this drama is a part of the brain named for its almond-like shape: the amygdala. The amygdala was discovered and named in the 1980s, and it later turned out to encompass more than the almond-shaped structure initially observed, but by then the name was so established that the scientific community chose not to change it.

The amygdala serves several essential functions: it's important for our memories and feelings and not least for how we interpret the feelings of others. But perhaps its most important task is to be on constant lookout for threats in our surroundings and to sound the alarm at the slightest detection. This means activating our stress system, i.e., the HPA axis. The way the amygdala works is known as the "smoke detector principle"—it's better to sound the alarm one time too many than one time too few. It's quick but not very accurate. In the middle of our hike, my amygdala noticed something that could have been a snake and immediately hit the button to make me freeze. *Better safe than sorry.*

THE RIGHT AMOUNT OF STRESS

The word "stress" brings to mind something negative, but we need stress in order to function. Short-term stress keeps us focused and sharpens our mental functions. In other words, there is no harm in having a tough day or week at work.

The importance of the body's stress system for normal functioning can be seen by studying what happens to lab animals when the HPA axis is disabled. The animals behave apathetically and have no energy; some of them even stop eating. A similar pattern can occasionally be observed in people with burnout—a condition of immense exhaustion where sometimes you can't even get out of bed because the HPA axis is no longer activating normally. Most likely it has been run into the ground by being under too much pressure for too long.

As you saw at the beginning of the book, almost every generation of humans that came before us lived in a perilous world where half of them didn't survive to their tenth birthday. From a historical

THE ATTENTION FIX

perspective, the smoke detector principle has been vital. A person who runs away from anything that resembles a lion has a better chance of survival than someone who just stands there. What does one time too many matter if one time too few could mean death? In other words, the amygdala is hasty for a reason.

Always engaged

Your amygdala is always engaged—not only when you feel threatened. Even now, as you read or listen to this book, your amygdala is scanning your surroundings without you being aware of it. So, isn't it a good thing that the amygdala is on the lookout for danger? Sure, but the problem is that just about anything can set it off: a loud noise in the street, being late for a meeting, not finishing a presentation on time or not getting enough likes on your latest Instagram post. The amygdala can respond to anything! The more stimuli there are around us, the more there is to set it off.

Certain things trigger the amygdala in just about everyone, including snakes, spiders, heights and confined spaces. This may seem odd, since it's extremely rare for people to die from a snake or spider bite, while in Europe 17,500 people die in traffic-related accidents and more than 700,000 as a result of smoking every year. The amygdala should react to cigarettes and driving without a seatbelt, but instead it's set off by snakes, spiders and heights. Why is that? Well, these things have claimed the lives of our ancestors for thousands of generations. From an evolutionary perspective, the amygdala has not yet had time to adapt to the threats of cars and smoking. That city dwellers are more likely to seek help from a psychologist for a snake or spider phobia than for a car phobia thus has a logical explanation and indicates a clear mismatch between the world we have evolved for and the one we live in.

Anxiety—arising from a *potential* threat

Anxiety. The word alone is enough to make me uneasy. But what exactly is anxiety? Well, in essence it's a survival mechanism, which can be hard to grasp if you have experienced severe anxiety. It's a feeling of intense discomfort that arises when we perceive something as a potential threat and the body's stress system kicks into gear.

Let's say you've been working hard to get into a university as a mature student and recently taken the entrance exam. The results have just been posted on the university's website, so you log on and search nervously for your name and . . . you failed. *No! No! No!* Both your heart and your mind are racing: *I've already handed in my notice at work and even found somewhere to live! What's everyone going to say?* At this point, you feel a lot of *stress*. Your heart beats faster and harder to deliver more blood to your muscles that need to perform at their best when you are facing danger. Even though it won't affect the exam results one bit, it's clear that your body is preparing for either fight or flight.

STAGE FRIGHT

What stresses you out more than anything? Perhaps it's speaking in front of others. For many, this is so stressful it even has a name: glossophobia. The explanation for why it's uncomfortable

---

to have everyone's eyes on you is probably that, for almost all of our evolution, it's been extremely important not to be excluded from the group. To prepare for what *might* happen if you are evaluated and socially humiliated—and thus ousted from the group—your brain fires up the stress system and your heart begins to pound.

Our innate sensitivity to being evaluated by other people is another example of our brain not being adapted to the modern world. If we give a bad presentation at work, we are unlikely to lose our job and thus risk starving to death. But in the world we long ago evolved for, exclusion from the group could be a matter of life and death. Belonging was not merely a matter of safety but also of survival. You simply couldn't make it on your own.

Now let's rewind a few weeks to the days before you took the exam. You were sleeping poorly, had little appetite and felt generally unsettled. You couldn't stop thinking about what would happen if you were to fail. That's *anxiety*. Which system is running in your body? The HPA axis, of course! The same fight-or-flight mechanism is activated in the case of both anxiety and stress, but for different reasons.

Stress is *a reaction to something that* is *a threat; anxiety, however, is a*

*reaction to something that we perceive *to be a threat.*

In other words, stress helps us face danger—but why do we have anxiety? Wouldn't it be better to feel fantastic until the exam? Turns out, it's not really that simple. Anxiety helps us plan and focus on what's important. If you tell yourself it'll work out and you watch Netflix instead of studying, your chances of passing the exam won't exactly improve.

Even illogical anxiety is logical

It's easy to see why someone might feel anxious about failing an important test, but even things that are wholly unlikely can cause anxiety: *What if the plane crashes?* Many people with anxiety imagine an array of more or less—usually less—likely disasters that may befall them. Some feel a vague worry that they can't link to anything external; it's just there, gnawing away at them. They know their worry is unjustified, yet they can't shake the feeling.

The reason why some people seem actively to look for things to worry about is that it has historically paid off for the stress system to be triggered at the slightest hint of danger—the so-called smoke detector principle. But today, our stress system is triggered unnecessarily for completely different reasons. When the person you fancy doesn't respond quickly enough to a text message, you think: *They don't like me, I'm worthless and will never meet someone.* And the HPA axis kicks into gear, ready to face the dangers of impending social exclusion.

In essence, it's the same as thinking that the rustling in the bush might be a snake with the HPA axis kicking in to make you run away—when you might just assume it's the wind and therefore nothing to worry about. "Better safe than sorry" were words to live by in our ancestors' world, but they aren't anymore.

Depression—a natural protection?

One million, one hundred and forty-nine thousand, nine hundred and forty-eight. I initially assume I must have misread it, but I haven't. The National Board of Health and Welfare's database states that, as of March 2023, more than 1.1 million Swedes over the age of 15 take antidepressants. That's more than *one in eight* adults in Sweden, and in the US the proportion is the same. Despite living longer, being healthier and having all the world's entertainment at our fingertips, we seem to be more depressed than ever. How did it come to this?

ANXIETY IS UNIQUELY HUMAN

The HPA axis plays a crucial role in how dogs, cats, rats and other animals respond to stress and threats, but they don't use it the way we do. No matter how hard you try, you will never get a rat to trigger its HPA axis at the thought that there might be more cats in the area next summer. No great white shark will release even the slightest amount of cortisol at the thought that, as a result of global warming, the seal population is in

---

danger of dwindling over the next decade. Yet such hypothetical scenarios do trigger the HPA axis in humans: *What if I don't pass the exam? What if I can't get the presentation right at work? What if my wife leaves me?*

The human ability to foresee the future is perhaps our most vital quality, but with it comes the ability also to see that which we want to avoid. That the stress system can go into overdrive because we *might* get fired, we *might* get divorced or we *might* not be able to pay the mortgage on our house is the price we pay for our intelligence. The brain struggles to distinguish real threats from imagined ones.

Anxiety means triggering the stress system preemptively. Now, the body being proactive is nothing out of the ordinary. If you are lying on the sofa, about to stand up, your blood pressure will rise before you get to your feet, otherwise you might feel dizzy. Anxiety can be viewed the same way—as the body triggering the stress system in advance.

A person who walks around with anxiety has a stress system that is always activated—if not fully, then at least constantly simmering, ready to face danger when it arises. As a result, the body constantly wants to be on the move and to get away from where you are. This can lead to several things, including:

Mental restlessness. A vague feeling of always wanting to be elsewhere that's not caused by boredom or curiosity. You don't want to stay where you are—no matter where that is. You end meetings early so you can leave the room. You eat fast so you can leave the table. You end your phone calls before they have even started. Onward, onward, onward.

Physical restlessness. The muscles in your body are set for fight or flight, but there is nothing to flee from or fight against. Yet your muscles still want to move and you struggle to be still. You fidget with things: twisting strands of your hair, tapping your foot against the floor, tensing the muscles in your neck and back until they are sore. At night, you clench your jaw muscles and grind your teeth.

Fatigue. Walking around on constant alert is energy sapping. As a result, you feel exhausted and completely worn out when you get home from school or work.

An upset stomach. If the body is in fight-or-flight mode, it won't bother with digestion, prioritizing other functions instead. After all, there isn't much point in digesting your food if you are about to become someone else's lunch.

Nausea. Have you ever tried to run fast right after a meal? It rarely works well with a stomach full of food. When anxiety and high stress levels make you nauseous, it's because your body is trying to get rid of the food in your stomach to enable you to fight or run away. This is why many actors and performers feel so nervous before a premiere or concert that they almost throw up.

Dry mouth. As your body prepares for battle, blood rushes to your muscles to provide them with more oxygen and nutrients to perform at their best. The three salivary glands in your mouth, which extract saliva by drawing fluid from the blood, thus have less blood to make saliva from—resulting in a dry mouth.

Sweating. A body that is about to fight or flee will get hot, and in order to cool down we begin to sweat. When the body expects to perform at its best, it tries to cool itself down.

During the spring, my job as an IT consultant was extremely stressful. On top of that, our son had mental health problems and didn't go to school, while we had bought a house without having sold our apartment, so we were under financial pressure, too. I slept terribly and didn't feel good at all, but I was still functioning. Around midsummer, everything finally fell into place: the apartment was sold, our son got the right help and things calmed down at work.

When our family went to Spain for a couple of weeks' long-awaited vacation, I immediately noticed something was wrong. I could hardly get out of bed and felt like my head was filled with cotton balls. Nothing was fun. Everything felt so bleak. All I wanted was to sleep, and I did—for 14–15 hours a day. Still, I didn't feel rested. When I got home, I contacted my doctor's office and after an ECG and some blood tests, I received my diagnosis: burnout. I was flabbergasted. The stress was over! Why now, when things had settled down?

Depression like the kind that affected my patient may seem illogical, even historically. It's easy to see that anxiety has helped us survive. But people who are depressed tend to withdraw, eat less, isolate themselves from others and lose interest in sex. All this means reducing your chances of surviving and passing on your genes. But why does depression often *follow* a period of stress?

The price of prolonged stress

The most common cause of depression is prolonged stress. For you and me, stress is usually caused by the difficulty of managing life. But for our ancestors, it wasn't an overflowing inbox or a bathroom renovation gone wrong that triggered their stress system. Instead, it was predators, people who wanted to kill them, starvation or infections. Those who were under a lot of stress for a long time probably found themselves in a world full of dangers—and that lives on in you and me.

The brain interprets high stress levels to mean that there are dangers everywhere. If so, there is a point in making sure you withdraw and pull the covers over your head. What tools does the brain have to guide us? Our feelings, of course! The brain tries to steer us away from what it interprets as a world full of dangers by controlling the way we feel, making us depressed so that we will isolate ourselves.

If the brain were perfectly adapted to today's world, prolonged stress would make us perform even better. After all, the problems causing my patient stress are not solved by pulling the covers over his head. The brain, however, pays no mind to this logic; it didn't evolve in today's world. Instead, its solution is to withdraw, because the brain interprets stress as the world being dangerous—which is what stress has meant for almost all of our time on earth.

You would be wise to think this sounds speculative. We should be careful about giving airtight evolutionary explanations for our feelings and behaviors. But there are a few clues to support the thesis that depression could be one of the brain's strategies for protecting us from a dangerous world. One such clue comes from an unexpected place: our immune system.

Depression—protecting us against infections?

Your genes influence your risk of becoming depressed, but there is no single "depression gene." Instead, hundreds of different genes make small contributions. These genes don't dictate whether you will ever be depressed, but they can make you more or less *vulnerable* to depression. In researching which genes these are, a remarkable discovery has been made: several genes that contribute to increasing your risk of depression also activate your immune system. This unexpected genetic link between depression and the body's immune system begs the question of whether depression could be the brain's way of protecting us from infection.

It may sound far-fetched to you and me—after all, if we get a bacterial infection, we just take antibiotics. But antibiotics are new. Penicillin was only discovered in 1928; as recently as the early 1900s, one in three children in the US died before the age of five. The top causes of death at the turn of the twentieth century were pneumonia, influenza, tuberculosis and diarrhea—all of which are caused by infectious diseases. Going back to the days of our ancestors, the mortality rate from infections is believed to have been even higher. A person injured while hunting could not only bleed to death but also risked dying if the wound became infected.

So, it's only natural that evolution has built in a range of mechanisms to protect us from infection. One is our powerful immune system; another is that we feel a strong distaste for food that's gone bad, to prevent us from putting it in our mouths—a "behavioral immune system." Yet another mechanism is our tendency to withdraw from situations where we are at risk of infection and injury. This could be the bridge between depression and infection. Several genes that affect the risk of depression seem to serve two functions: firstly, to kick-start our immune system; and secondly, to keep us away from dangers, injuries and infections. The latter they achieve by making us depressed.

However, these genes are activated not only when we are injured but also when we are *at risk* of being injured, as they ensure that the immune system is activated and ready to face both bacteria and viruses. Where are we at risk of being injured? In a world full of threats, of course! And what is it that signals to our brains that there are many threats around? You guessed it—our high stress levels!

Important to put your feelings into words

So, my patient who became depressed while on vacation, after a period of intense stress, may have a brain that was trying to protect him from danger, infection and being beaten to death. When he was lying in his hotel room, feeling as though life was hopeless, his brain was solving a series of evolutionary problems faced by our ancestors—though I understand that, for him and all others affected, it probably comes as cold comfort that depression may in fact have evolved to help us.

As a psychiatrist, I have found it valuable for my patients to gain an understanding of the role their feelings can play. When they realize that anxiety has saved us from dangers and that depression may protect us against infections and conflict, they can think to themselves: *It's not my fault that I'm depressed. My brain is just doing what it has evolved to do in a world that looked different from the one I live in. Being depressed is entirely natural.*

Warning signs

There is another reason why you should know that prolonged stress can lead to depression, and how stress basically means that the body is prioritizing fight or flight over digestion, sleep, mood and sex drive. Most people who suffer from severe effects of stress have been given several warnings in the form of trouble sleeping, stomach problems, susceptibility to infection, teeth grinding, short-term memory loss and irritability. Why have they ignored these red flags?

My understanding is that they haven't understood them as warning signs. They haven't made the connection between their symptoms and stress. This is a shame, because if you can pump the brakes in time, you have a good chance of avoiding, say, full-blown depression. Stress-related issues, including depression, are much easier to prevent than treat, and stress symptoms can therefore be a godsend. Understanding what stress really is and how it might manifest gives us an opportunity to slow down before it's too late.

It's not always the "fittest" who survive

One of the genes that increases the risk of depression is central to the substance serotonin in the brain and tends to make people more sensitive to stress. If you artificially remove this gene from mice, they tolerate stress better. You might wonder why such a gene exists at all and why evolution hasn't removed it. Most likely the answer is that the fittest, smartest or most stress-resistant individual is not always the one who survives. It's been at least as important to avoid danger and conflict, cope with infection and not starve to death in a world where food was scarce. This is probably a big reason why so many people suffer from depression and anxiety—it has quite simply helped us survive.

I hope you have gained a greater understanding of the role played by our feelings, why anxiety and depression may have been crucial to our survival and how the body's stress system is designed to protect us in a lethal world. Now it's time to have a look at the implications of these circumstances in our modern, connected world.

CHAPTER 3

CELL PHONES—OUR NEW DRUG

How do we consume as much of your time and conscious attention
as possible? We exploited a vulnerability in human psychology.
We give you a little dopamine hit.

SEAN PARKER, FORMER PRESIDENT AND BOARD
MEMBER OF FACEBOOK

IF YOU DON'T HAVE your phone in sight, I'm sure you know where it is—otherwise you probably wouldn't be able to concentrate on these words. The first thing we do when we wake up in the morning is reach for our phone, and the last thing we do is put it on our bedside table. We touch—swipe, type or tap—our phone more than 2,600 times a day, picking it up on average every ten minutes—every waking hour. In fact, our waking hours don't seem to be enough;

one in three people (50 percent of all 18–24-year-olds) check their phone at least once in the middle of the night, too.

If we lose our phone, our world collapses—40 percent of us would rather be without our voice for a whole day than our phone (yes, it's true!). Everywhere we look, in the street, in cafes, in restaurants, on the bus, at the dinner table—even at the gym—everyone is staring down at their phone. Whether we like it or not, we have become addicted! But to understand how cell phones and screens have managed to seduce an entire world, let's peek inside the brain once more.

The role of dopamine

If you wanted to write a book about one of the brain's messenger substances, dopamine wouldn't be a bad choice. It's also key to understanding why cell phones are so seductive. Dopamine is often described as a reward molecule, but that's not the whole truth. Its most important task is not to make us feel good but to make us choose what to focus on. Dopamine is our engine.

When you are hungry and someone puts food on the table, your dopamine levels rise just by looking at it. In other words, it's not when you eat the food that your dopamine increases. Dopamine makes you want to eat the food and tells you: *This is what you should focus on*. But if dopamine motivates us to do things, rather than giving us feelings of pleasure, then where do the latter come from? Endorphins, "the body's own morphine," play an important role. While dopamine makes you want to eat the yummy food in front of you, it's endorphins that make it taste good.

Dopamine plays an important role in the brain's reward system, which—like the stress system—has evolved over millions of years. And for both of these systems, today's society is an alien world. The reward system steers us toward behaviors that help us survive and pass on our genes. In other words, it's not surprising that food, socializing—important for pack animals like humans—and sex raise our dopamine levels. Cell phones make our dopamine rise too, which is why you feel a strong urge to pick yours up when you get a text message. In fact, the cell phone has managed to hack a number of basic mechanisms in our reward system. Let's take a closer look at how.

We love the new

From an evolutionary perspective, it's no wonder that humans are hungry for knowledge. By learning more about the world around us, we improve our chances of survival. Someone who knows how weather changes affect lion behavior or in which situations antelopes are the most distracted, allowing you to sneak up on them, has a better chance of both succeeding in the hunt and avoiding becoming a predator's dinner.

From birth, we have a hardwired urge to seek out the new and unknown, which contributes to our desire to see new places, meet new people and experience new things.

The implication of this principle—that the more we know about the world around us, the more likely we are to survive—is that nature has endowed us with an instinct to seek out new information. You can probably guess which substance in the brain is behind this instinct: dopamine, of course! When you learn something new, the brain releases dopamine.

The brain not only craves new information, it also wants novelty in the form of new environments and experiences. The brain has dopamine-producing cells that seem to only respond to new things. If you see something you recognize, like the street you live on, they won't respond. If you see something new, however, like an unfamiliar face, the cells are suddenly activated. The same thing happens if you see something emotionally charged.

The presence of dopamine cells thirsting for new information—including new environments—means that the brain rewards novelty. From birth, we have a hardwired urge to seek out the new and unknown, which contributes to our desire to see new places, meet new people and experience new things. Presumably this drive was a way to motivate our ancestors to explore new possibilities in a world where food and resources were scarce.

Let's jump back 100,000 years and imagine two women trying to solve the eternal problem of finding food. One has a drive to seek out the new—to explore new areas and environments—while the other lacks the same drive. I think the former has a better chance of finding food. The more ground you cover, the more likely you are to find something edible.

Now let's fast-forward to you and me. Our brains remain largely unchanged, so the desire for new things lives on inside us, only now it's expressed in forms other than simply a longing to see other places. It leads instead to a craving for new knowledge and information delivered by our computers and phones. With each new page on the screen, our brains release dopamine—and as a result we like to keep clicking, tapping, swiping, scrolling. We really do seem to like the next page better than the one we are currently on, so much so that we spend less than four seconds on almost one-fifth of all the pages we visit. Only on 4 percent do we stay for more than ten minutes.

When we acquire new information—because that's essentially what we are doing, whether it's checking a news site, our email or social media—the reward system is activated in the same way as when our ancestors saw new places and environments. In fact, reward-seeking behaviors are so close to information-seeking behaviors in the brain that it's sometimes difficult to separate them.

The brain loves "maybe"

However, it's not money, food, sex, validation or new experiences that trigger our reward system the most, but the expectation of these. Nothing kicks our reward center into gear like something that *might* happen. In the 1930s, scientists discovered that rats that were fed when they pushed a lever would push more often if it only *sometimes* led to food. They were most eager if they were fed 30–70 percent of the time.

A couple of decades later, an experiment was carried out in which monkeys were played a certain sound and then given a sip of juice. Eventually, it turned out that the monkeys' dopamine levels rose just from hearing the sound—and significantly more so than when they drank the juice. The experiment shows that dopamine isn't a "reward molecule" that provides pleasure; rather it tells us what to focus our attention on. The same researchers also found that the dopamine rose even more if the sound was only *sometimes* followed by a sip of juice. Every other time was the reward frequency that elicited the most dopamine.

The same phenomenon observed in rats was also seen in monkeys—and it applies to humans, too. In an experiment where the participants were told to pick a card that could pay out money, their dopamine levels rose less if they were guaranteed money each time than if the payout was uncertain. And just like in rats and monkeys, giving the reward every other time increased their dopamine levels the most. For the brain, then, the "journey" is the reward, where the journey is the *expectation* of a future—uncertain—reward.

Shouldn't we like certainty more than uncertainty? Why the brain rewards uncertain outcomes with more dopamine is impossible to say with complete confidence, but the most likely explanation is that dopamine's main task is to motivate us.

"Maybe" creates a craving for your phone!

Imagine one of your foremothers standing in front of a group of trees that only sometimes bear fruit. Since the fruit is not visible from the ground, she must climb up into a tree to see if it has any. If it's empty, it's important that she keeps looking and climbs other trees as well. A person who doesn't give up after drawing a blank is eventually rewarded with high-calorie fruit—and better chances of survival.

Most processes in nature are unpredictable—just like trees that sometimes bear fruit. You don't know in advance if you will be rewarded. Our dopamine levels spiking in the face of an uncertain outcome could serve the same function as them spiking in the face of novelty—it keeps us looking even when we don't know if we will be rewarded. Presumably this drive helped our ancestors discover and exploit the limited resources available in a world where food was scarce.

Today, our built-in predilection for unknown outcomes can cause problems, like making us stay at slot machines and casino tables. Everyone knows that in the long run the house always wins, yet we gamble anyway. One reason is probably sheer entertainment value, but some find it so difficult to control their gambling that they develop an addiction. Considering the tendency of the brain's reward system to over-reward uncertain outcomes, it's no wonder that games of chance, and the potential rewards they offer, can be so seductive. *Just one more round of poker; this time it could be my turn to win.*

Gambling companies and casinos aren't the only ones exploiting this mechanism in our brains. It's also an important reason why you feel a strong urge to pick up your phone when it dings with a text message or email—after all, it could be something important. In most cases, your dopamine levels rise more when you hear the signal than when you read the email or text message itself. The powerful idea that it *might* be important urges us to pick up our phones "just to check." And we do it often. Every ten minutes, for all our waking hours.

Social media triggers our reward center

Besides gambling companies and cell phone manufacturers, there are other companies that are particularly adept at exploiting our love of unknown outcomes: social media platforms. Facebook, Instagram and Snapchat all create an urge to pick up your phone and check if there might be some important update or a new like in your feed. What's more, they serve up their digital validation when your reward system is at its most triggered. Often, the like on your vacation photo doesn't pop up the same second that someone clicks on the thumbs-up. Sometimes Facebook and Instagram withhold their likes because they want to wait until your reward system will be maximally triggered. By dividing the stimuli into small portions, they maximize the expectation of a digital reward.

Social media developers have studied our reward system closely and are well aware of the brain's love of uncertain outcomes, as well as how frequent they should be. They use their knowledge to create elements of surprise that will make us want to pick up our phones all the time. *Maybe I got another like, I'd better check* is the same mechanism at work as *Just one more round of poker; this time I might get lucky.*

WHO GETS ADDICTED TO THEIR PHONE?

On average, we use our cell phones for three hours a day. Of course, some people spend less time than that on their phones and others even more. Is there anything that distinguishes those who use it the most? When researchers examined the cell phone habits of nearly 700 university students, they found that one-third were so addicted that they couldn't stay off their phones even at night, which left them tired during the day. Among the "big consumers" were mainly individuals with type A personality traits: competitive people with low self-esteem who put themselves under a lot of pressure. People with a more laid-back and relaxed attitude to life—type B personalities—generally didn't have the same problems with phone addiction.

Many of these companies have hired behavioral and brain scientists to ensure that their apps tap into the brain's reward system as efficiently as possible and become maximally addictive. Further, these companies have hundreds of millions of users and can take a small group of these and test how different ways of distributing likes, hearts or thumbs-up affect how much time we spend in the app. The most efficient way of distributing the digital rewards, that maximizes both how often we log in and the time we spend, are rolled out to everyone. From a crassly economic perspective, developers have no doubt been successful in hacking our brains.

Silicon Valley's pang of conscience

Those most intimately familiar with the technology seem to realize that it is so seductive they would be wise to limit it. Justin Rosenstein, an American in his thirties, decided to put restrictions on his

Facebook usage and quit Snapchat altogether, which he compared to heroin in its capacity to create addiction. To curb his cell phone use, he installed a feature designed to help parents limit their children's phone habits.

Rosenstein's actions are particularly interesting as he was the one who created the "like" button on Facebook. In other words, the man behind the digital thumbs-up thinks that his own creation is far too alluring, and in an interview he seemed almost rueful: "It is very common for humans to develop things with the best of intentions and for them to have unintended, negative consequences."

He is not alone in Silicon Valley in holding such views. Tony Fadell, one of the Apple executives who helped develop the iPad, had similar thoughts when he saw the power it has over children.

I wake up in cold sweats, thinking, "What did we bring to the world?" . . . And I know when I take [technology] away from my kids what happens. They literally feel like you're tearing a piece of their person away from them—they get emotional about it, very emotional. They go through withdrawal for two to three days.

"Low-tech parent"

The most telling example of a tech leader's ambivalence toward his own product, however, was Apple's own founder, Steve Jobs. At a convention in San Francisco in early 2010, he showed off the iPad to a blissful audience for the first time. He heaped superlatives on the tablet, calling it "a magical and revolutionary device."

What he didn't mention was his caution about letting his own children use it, as he felt it was too addictive. In an interview, a *New York Times* reporter recalls asking Jobs if, at home, his walls were giant touch screens, and iPads and iPods were handed out to guests like chocolates on a pillow. "Not even close," Jobs replied, and explained that screen time was strictly limited. The dumbfounded journalist concluded that Jobs was a "low-tech parent."

Few have had a more astute sense of how technology affects us than Steve Jobs. Over the course of a decade, he launched a series of products that changed the way we consume films, music and magazine articles, not to mention the way we communicate with each other. Jobs's caution about letting his children use the technology says more than most research studies and opinion pieces.

In Sweden, one in three children between two and three years old use a tablet every day, at an age when they haven't even learned to talk properly. Meanwhile, Steve Jobs's teenage children had tough restrictions on how much they were allowed to use their iPads. He seems to have been one step ahead of everyone else, not only in developing the technology but also in understanding its effects on us.

Steve Jobs is not an outlier among our most influential tech leaders. Bill Gates revealed that his children did not get their own cell phones until they turned 14. Today, 91 percent of American 14-year-olds have their own phone. Bill Gates's children would thus have been among the 9 percent who did not—which could hardly be attributed to Gates not being able to meet the expense.

Easy to get swept up in the digital merry-go-round

You are busy writing a report at work when you hear your phone ding with a new text message and you feel a strong urge to pick it up—after all, it *could* be important. While you have your phone in hand, you pop onto Facebook to see if you have any new likes on your latest post.

You notice that someone has shared an article about the rising crime rate in your area. You click on the article but only have time to read a few lines before a link to a page with cut-price sneakers grabs your eye. After little more than a quick glance, however, you are interrupted by a push notification about a new Instagram post from one of your best friends. Suddenly, the report you are writing is far from your mind.

Your brain is doing exactly what it has evolved to do over hundreds of thousands of years. It rewards uncertain outcomes—the text message—with dopamine, making you feel a strong urge to look at your phone. Your brain is searching for new information, especially the kind that's emotionally charged and linked to danger: the article about crime. It provides a sense of social interaction: the push notification. It lets you focus on how others have reacted to you telling them about yourself: liking your post.

A series of mechanisms, all of which have been the brain's survival strategies, ensure that you are thrown from one digital distraction to the next. The brain doesn't give two hoots that it is preventing you from writing your report; it didn't evolve to write reports but to help your ancestors survive.

Now you have a better sense of the mechanisms in the brain that your cell phone was designed to "hack" and why it's so hard to put it down. But how are we affected by the unparalleled ability of phones to keep us spellbound? That's what we'll look at next.

CHAPTER 4

FOCUS—THE SCARCITY OF OUR TIME

People can't do [multitasking] very well and when they say they can, they're deluding themselves.

EARL MILLER, PROFESSOR OF NEUROSCIENCE AT MASSACHUSETTS INSTITUTE OF TECHNOLOGY

HAVE YOU NOTICED IN recent years that you have been trying to do more things at the same time? If so, you are far from alone. Personally, I find it difficult simply to watch a film. I have noticed that I often reach for my phone to check emails or browse aimlessly while trying to keep up with the plot.

More than anything, our digital lifestyle means that we often try to do several things at once—that is, multitask. Researchers at Stanford University decided to investigate how good multitaskers are at various mental tasks and gathered nearly 300 volunteers. Half of them felt they had no problems whatsoever browsing different websites while studying. The other half preferred to do one thing at a time. After a series of tests examining their ability to concentrate, the multitaskers were found to be less able to focus. Much less. In particular, they struggled to ignore irrelevant information, which they couldn't filter out. They seemed to be distracted by everything.

The same poor results were observed when the memory of these multitaskers was tested in an experiment in which they had to hold a series of letters in their mind. *But surely they must be better at something*, the researchers thought, and decided to test their ability to quickly jump from one task to another—i.e., to multitask. But even at their own game—multitasking—the multitaskers were beat!

The price of multitasking

The brain has an incredible ability to handle a wide range of processes in parallel, but there is one area in which our mental bandwidth is severely limited: our attention. We simply cannot focus on more than one thing at a time.

What we are actually doing when we think we are multitasking is jumping quickly between tasks.

When you are listening to a lecture while also writing an email—and feeling impressed by your own ability to do both at the same time—the truth is that you are switching quickly between the two. And while shifting focus may only take a tenth of a second, the problem is that your brain lingers on what you just did. When you turn your attention to your email, your brain will continue to dedicate some of its bandwidth to the lecturer. The same happens when you switch from writing emails to listening to the lecture.

The fact that the brain has a transition period and lingers on what you were just doing is known in scientific language as "attention residue." When you think you are only spending a few seconds on your emails, the price is actually higher. It's not possible to say exactly how long this transition period lasts, but studies suggest that it takes several minutes for the brain to focus 100 percent on a task after a change of focus.

Not *everyone* is bad at multitasking, however. There are actually those who *can* do several things in parallel. They are a small group sometimes referred to as "super-multitaskers." It's believed that a few percent of the population have this trait. But for the vast majority, the brain *doesn't* work that way. Interestingly, women generally seem to be better at multitasking than men.

The brain rewards itself when it underperforms

When we are trying to do several things at once but are actually jumping from one task to another, the brain isn't working very efficiently. The fact that the brain is a lousy juggler, fumbling and dropping all the balls, should discourage us from multitasking. Yet it doesn't. Instead, when we multitask, it rewards us with dopamine, which makes us feel good. In other words, the brain tries to motivate us to do something that makes it underperform. Why would that be?

The reason we feel good when shifting our attention between different things may be that our ancestors needed to stay alert in order to react quickly to any stimuli around them. The slightest distraction could mean danger, so it was important not to miss anything—hence the smoke detector principle! A split focus and the ability to react swiftly to anything that came our way may have been vital at a time when life was so dangerous that half of all people died before their tenth birthday. This has been the basis for the brain's evolution and is why it rewards itself with dopamine in order to motivate us to multitask and be easily distracted. We like it, but it comes at a price.

Our limited working memory

Multitasking doesn't only impair our concentration; it also seems to affect our working memory, which acts as a "mental workbench" where we keep what we are doing in our heads. Let's say you are about to call a phone number that you have written down on a piece of paper. You look at the note, memorize the number and dial it. The number resides in your working memory, which—like your ability to concentrate—is strictly limited. For this reason, most people can only hold six to seven digits in their heads. Personally, I can't even manage that, and get annoyed every time I have to double-check that I'm typing the right phone number or email address.

In an experiment involving 150 teenagers, some of whom were used to multitasking, a series of sentences was displayed on a screen. Some were perfectly correct, like "For breakfast I had a cheese sandwich," while others contained gibberish: "For breakfast I had a plate of shoelaces." The task was to indicate which were correct. It may sound easy, but the participants had to be quick—the sentences were only displayed for two seconds. What's more, there was other, distracting information being displayed on the screen that had to be ignored. Solving the task required a good working memory.

The results? The multitaskers performed worse: their working memory was poorer than the others'. In particular, they seemed to struggle to ignore the distracting information next to the sentences. Their frontal lobe was also found to be more active. One of the most important tasks of the frontal lobe is to ensure that we stay focused. That it appeared to be working harder could be compared to how a strong person can lift a chair with only one arm, while someone who isn't quite as brawny needs to use both. In other words, for multi-taskers to keep their focus, the frontal lobe is forced to recruit more mental resources. Yet despite its increased effort, the multitaskers' final results were still worse!

The researchers behind the study concluded that people who multitask a lot seem to struggle to sort out and ignore irrelevant information: "Constant distractions seem to almost guarantee that the brain will not function optimally."

Your phone distracts even on silent

Both our concentration and our working memory seem to be negatively affected by trying to do several things at once. Now, you are probably thinking that this means we just have to turn off our computers and leave our phones on silent in our pockets. Unfortunately, it's not that simple. As you saw in the last chapter, cell phones have an almost unparalleled ability to attract our attention, and that doesn't seem to cease just because we put them down.

When the memory and concentration of 500 university students were tested, those who had to leave their cell phone outside the testing room performed better than those who had it on silent in their pocket. The test subjects had no idea that the presence of their phone was affecting them, but the results spoke for themselves—they were distracted merely by having it on their person. The same phenomenon has been observed in several other studies. In one, 800 people were asked to perform a series of high-concentration exercises on a computer. Afterward, it turned out that those who had left their cell phone in another room performed better than those who had it on silent in their pocket. To find out the results, it's enough to read the title of the research report: "Brain drain: the mere presence of one's own smartphone reduces available cognitive capacity."

Japanese researchers came to a similar conclusion when they asked a group of study participants to complete an attention-demanding task in which they had to find a number of hidden characters on a screen as quickly as possible. Half had a cell phone that was not theirs lying next to the screen, which they weren't allowed to pick up. The other half had a small notepad lying on the table. The results? Those with the notepad did best. The phone seemed to steal the subjects' attention just by lying there.

Ignoring your phone is an active choice

On a subconscious level, the brain seems to be aware of the digital draw of the phone in your pocket and has to spend a certain amount of mental bandwidth ignoring it. As a result, your concentration isn't what it could be. If you think about it, it's not very surprising.

Dopamine tells your brain what's important and what you should focus on. Your phone triggering a release of dopamine hundreds of times a day will no doubt make you more interested in it.

Ignoring something is an active choice that requires the brain to make an effort. You have probably noticed it yourself. When you are sitting down for coffee with a friend, you put your phone on the table—perhaps screen down to avoid distraction. Once you are sitting there, in order to resist the impulse to pick it up, you have to keep thinking: *I'm not going to pick up my phone.* It's not surprising that your brain has to expend mental capacity ignoring something that serves up hundreds of little dopamine hits a day. After all, it has evolved to seek out anything that provides more dopamine.

When the brain has to put effort into resisting the pull of your phone, its capacity to perform other tasks decreases. It probably won't matter much if what you are doing doesn't require a lot of focus. But if you really need to concentrate, it can be a problem. Like when American researchers had their test subjects take a demanding concentration test, during which some of them received a text message or phone call from the test leaders that they weren't supposed to answer. It turned out that they still made more mistakes on the test—three times as many, in fact!

The same effect was observed when a number of study participants were asked to read a text in a Word document with plain formatting followed by another text where some of the words had been turned into hyperlinks. Afterward, when they had to answer questions about the texts they had just read, it turned out they had learned less from the text with links, even though they didn't click on them. The explanation is probably that the brain constantly has to make a decision—*should I click on the link or not?*—and each small decision takes up mental bandwidth, sapping both our limited power of concentration and our working memory. Just as the brain has to expend energy in order not to pick up the phone on the table, it takes energy not to click on the link.

We train ourselves to become even more distracted

One might think that a heavy flow of information would train our concentration and that a brain exposed to digital distractions would gradually become more tolerant of them—the same way our muscles can withstand more strain if they are exercised through running or lifting weights. The problem is that most people's brains seem to work in precisely the opposite way. If anything, frequent diversions appear to make the brain even more easily distracted.

The digital distractions that constantly wash over us seem to make us even more sensitive to being disturbed. This could be one reason why so many people feel that in recent years it has become increasingly difficult to concentrate, even when they are not browsing the internet. Personally, I find that I struggle more and more to focus when reading a book. Nowadays, it's not enough just to put my phone on silent; I have to leave it in another room to concentrate. Even so, I often find it difficult to sink into a book the way I did ten years ago. If I get to a page that requires more focus, I feel a strong urge to reach for my phone, as though I don't have it in me to make the same effort anymore.

Many seem to have similar experiences. When distraction becomes the norm, we begin to crave it—even when it doesn't exist. Focus has become a scarcity in today's world. But the idea that our attention span has dropped from 12 to 8 seconds—and is now shorter than that of a goldfish—is thankfully just a myth.

Making knowledge stick

There are certain places where it's wise to be particularly careful with cell phones: in classrooms and lecture halls. For it's not only our concentration and working memory that they compromise, but also our ability to create long-term memories. If we have a cell phone or computer next to us, we learn less.

In a study, researchers had two groups of university students listen to a lecture. One group was allowed to bring computers, the other was not. When following up on what the group with computers had been doing in the lecture, it turned out that they had browsed some websites containing information related to the lecture—but they had also checked their email and Facebook. Immediately after the lecture, it was clear that those who'd had access to a computer didn't remember as much as the others. To make sure that the results weren't due to the composition of the groups, the same experiment was repeated with two new sets of students. But the results were the same: those without a computer learned more.

So, you might be thinking, *all we have to do is not go on Facebook during a lecture, right*? Sure, that would certainly help. But beyond the ability to browse social media, there may be other mechanisms through which the computer affects the way we absorb information. When American scientists had a group of students listen to a TED talk, some were asked to take notes with pen and paper, while others typed on their computers. Afterward, it turned out that those who had written on paper had understood the lecture better. They didn't necessarily remember more details, but they had a stronger grasp of the main point of the lecture. The results were summarized in the telling title: "The pen is mightier than the keyboard—advantages of longhand over laptop note taking."

Scientists are not sure why this is, but they speculate that those using a computer might just be typing what's being said word for word. With a pen, most people can't write as fast as they can with a keyboard, so we are forced to choose what to write down. This means that when we write by hand, we have to process the information and thus we absorb it better.

Interestingly, the mere presence of a cell phone seems to interfere more as time goes on. Participants who listened to a lecture and had their phones with them picked up as much information during the first 10–15 minutes as those who left their phones outside the lecture hall. But after that, they registered less and less of what was said. Perhaps it reflects the fact that when our concentration begins to flag—as it's prone to do after about 15 minutes of listening intently—the phone, in effect, becomes the drop that makes the metaphorical cup run over.

Focus is required to create long-term memories

When we learn something—that is, when we create a new memory—the connections between our brain cells change. To form a short-term memory, which lasts only a little while, the brain simply needs to strengthen already existing connections. Creating a long-term memory that will last for months, years or even a lifetime, however, is a more complex process. For that, the brain must create brand-new connections between brain cells. To make them last, so that the memory can be retained for a long time, new proteins must form.

But new proteins aren't enough; the brain must repeatedly run a signal through the newly formed pathway to strengthen it. This requires the brain to work hard and is an energy-intensive process. The creation of new long-term memories—known in scientific language as "consolidation"—is one of the brain's most energy-consuming processes. In part, it takes place when we sleep, and is probably an important reason why we sleep at all—as we shall return to a little later in this book.

Let's take a closer look at how consolidation works. Step one is focusing on something and thus telling the brain: *This is important and worth spending energy on—and creating a long-term memory.* If we don't focus our attention, the process won't work. The reason you can't remember where you left your keys when you came home from work yesterday is because you were distracted and had other things on your mind. Your brain didn't get the message that it was important and didn't memorize the location. Which is why, the next morning, you run around looking for your keys all over the house.

The same applies if you try to study for an exam in a noisy room; you will find it hard to concentrate. Your brain does not receive the message *This is important* and so you will have trouble remembering what you read. What this means, put simply, is that we can only withdraw from our memory what we deposit there. And in order for something to turn into a memory, we must concentrate.

The next step is to keep the information in our working memory—only then can the brain create a long-term memory through consolidation. Bombarding the brain with an endless stream of stimuli as we flit between Instagram, text messages, tweets, emails, news flashes and Facebook disrupts the process by which our impressions are turned into memories. And it can be disrupted in several ways.

Besides the brain's inability to focus when there is always something new happening, our limited working memory can become overloaded. When you try to study with the TV on in the background and while fiddling with your phone, your brain is forced to devote energy to processing all this information. That means it doesn't have time to create new long-term memories—and you don't learn what you read.

We fool ourselves into thinking that we are efficiently absorbing new information as we flit between different digital distractions. But the problem is that we are only bouncing on the surface and not allowing the information to sink in. And the drive that makes us do this is that we like it—after all, it releases dopamine.

In a study showing how our ability to create long-term memories is compromised by our digital habits, students were tasked with reading a chapter from a book at their own pace, before answering questions about the text. Meanwhile, some of them received a number of text messages on their phones that they needed to reply to. Since it took time to respond to the messages, it consequently took them longer to finish the reading. The study showed that all the students learned equally well, but those who were busy responding to messages took significantly longer. Even after deducting time to both read the messages and write a reply, it still took them longer to finish the chapter.

It thus appears to take time before you regain your full concentration and can return to where you left off—the brain has a so-called transition period. Trying to answer emails or text messages while studying may mean spending more time learning what you are reading—even after subtracting the time spent on your phone. In other words, if you are trying to multitask at work or while studying for an exam, you risk fooling yourself twice: you will learn less *and* need more time. So, it's a good idea to set aside a few minutes every hour to check your texts and emails, rather than trying always to keep an eye out for the second they show up.

The brain loves shortcuts

The brain is the body's most energy-intensive organ. In adults, the brain is responsible for 20 percent of the total daily energy consumption, and in teenagers that figure is around 30 percent. In newborns, 50 percent of all their energy goes to the brain! Even though you and I can fill up on as many calories as we want, almost all previous generations of humans couldn't. For this reason, the brain—like the rest of our body—is set up to conserve energy and do things as efficiently as possible. This means that it tries to take shortcuts, not least when it comes to memories, because creating memories requires a lot of energy.

This has consequences in our digital society. In one study, a number of people were asked to listen to a series of sentences that contained different types of facts, and after each sentence they were instructed to type it into a computer. Some were told that the computer saved the information, others that it was deleted. After they'd typed up all the sentences, they had to repeat as many as they could. It turned out that those who thought the computer had saved the information remembered fewer sentences than those who thought it had been deleted.

Why should I waste energy on this when it's being saved? the brain seems to argue, and it's not very surprising. If the brain can delegate a task to a computer, it's tempting to do so. Strangely, if we think something is being saved, we are more likely to remember *where* the information is than the content of the information. When test subjects were asked to type statements of fact into Word documents, one sentence per document, and save them in different folders, they couldn't remember many sentences the next day. However, they did remember in which folders they had put the documents!

The Google effect—not committing information to memory

It's called the "Google effect" or "digital amnesia," when the brain doesn't bother learning what it thinks is stored elsewhere. It prioritizes remembering *where* the information is, rather than the content of the information. But the Google effect doesn't just make it hard for us to remember facts. In one study, a group visiting an art museum was asked to photograph some of the artworks and just look at others. The next day, they were shown photos of a series of artworks; some they had seen in the museum, others they had not. The task was to try to remember if the art in the pictures was the same as in the museum.

It turned out that the participants had an easier time remembering the artworks they had *not* photographed; the others were harder to recall. Just as the brain doesn't bother to learn sentences stored on a computer, it doesn't bother memorizing what we have photographed. Instead, the brain takes a shortcut. *Why memorize the artwork itself when you can see it in a picture?*

So why should we bother learning anything at all when Google and Wikipedia are just a tap away on our phones? If it was only a matter of forgetting phone numbers, it wouldn't be a problem, but naturally we can't replace all our knowledge with Google. We need knowledge to be able to relate to the world, ask critical questions and evaluate information. Consolidation—when information is transferred from our short-term to our long-term memory—isn't simply moving "raw data" from the brain's RAM to its hard drive. It also involves integrating the information into our personal memories to build what we call "knowledge."

Human knowledge isn't the same as being able to reel off a long list of facts. The wisest person you know isn't necessarily the best at Trivial Pursuit. Truly learning something in depth requires both contemplation and focus. In a world of fast clicks, that's what we risk losing out on! If we are constantly jumping from one site to another, we aren't giving the brain time to digest the information.

Steve Jobs described the computer as a "bicycle for the mind"— a tool that allows us to think faster. In some ways, it's more accurate to call it "a cab driver for the mind"—it does the thinking for us. It's certainly convenient. But when it comes to learning new things, it might not be something we want to delegate to something else.

Losing interest in your surroundings

Every time I'm having coffee or a meal with someone and they pick up their phone, I get annoyed—but I'm no better! There is a selfish reason why you should try to avoid doing this, besides the fact that other people are likely to appreciate it. There is a risk that you will find the conversation itself more boring if you keep your phone in front of you. Turns out, our phones are so seductive that they seem to make us less interested in others.

In one study, 30 people were asked to meet a stranger for ten minutes and talk about anything they wanted. They each sat on a chair with a table between them. Some were allowed to keep their phones on the table, others weren't. Afterward, they were asked to describe how interesting they thought the conversation had been. Those who'd had their phones in sight found the conversation less interesting and even thought their interlocutors were less trustworthy and empathetic. And to be clear, their phones were just lying there—they didn't even pick them up!

WHEN MULTITASKING, MEMORIES ARE MISPLACED

Memories are stored in different parts of the brain. For example, facts and experiences are processed in the hippocampus, commonly known as the "memory center." When you learn a skill, on the other hand—such as riding a bike, swimming or perfecting a golf swing—another part, known as the striatum, is engaged. If we try to do several things at once, like watching TV and reading a book, the information will to a greater extent go to the striatum. In other words, multitasking makes the brain send information about facts to the wrong place. When you go back to just doing one thing, the information is suddenly sent to the hippocampus again.

Let's say that I'm remembering a walk in New York City where I had a tasty chocolate doughnut. The memory may have been evoked by being in New York again, eating a dough-nut somewhere else, wearing the same clothes, eating some other chocolate treat or inhabiting the same emotional state. The brain is brilliant at making associations, with the capacity to use small clues that are somehow reminiscent of an earlier event to retrieve the memory.

It seems that the ability to create flexible memories is partly lost when we try to do several things at once. And the reason is that the information goes not only to the hippocampus but also to the striatum. Memory tests often look at whether partici-pants can remember words and numbers, but our memory is more complex than that. Memories of factual information are mixed with our personal experiences, creating knowledge that we can twist and turn, look at from multiple angles and use to understand the world around us.

We don't yet know for sure how this incredibly complex system is affected by the flood of information pouring over us, but it could mean that digitization is affecting us on a deeper level than we know. What if something is lost along the way, something much more profound than how many numbers we can recite in a memory test?

This isn't particularly surprising either. After all, dopamine tells us where to focus our attention! If there is an object in front of us that serves up thousands of little dopamine hits every day, naturally the brain will be drawn there. When we must resist the impulse to pick up our phones, our limited concentration is disrupted—as we know, ignoring it is an active choice—with the consequence that we don't follow the conversation.

The same phenomenon was observed by researchers examining how 300 people perceived a dinner with friends. Half of them had been told they would receive a text message during dinner and should therefore have their phones at hand. The others were asked not to have their phones out. Afterward, it turned out that those who had kept their phones close found the dinner less rewarding. The differences weren't vast, but they were clear. Simply put, if you keep your phone on the table in front of you, you will find others just a bit less interesting.

But surely having your phone out while waiting for a text message shouldn't ruin a whole dinner? Perhaps not, though the people in the study didn't exactly leave their phone on standby. Rather, they fiddled with it for more than 10 percent of the total dinner time— even though they only needed to keep it in front of them to reply to a text message.

The role of dopamine is to tell us what's important and what we should focus on, where "important" isn't getting good grades, climbing the career ladder or even feeling well, but strictly what made our ancestors survive and pass on their genes. Something as ingeniously designed as a cell phone can provide a tiny dopamine hit 300 times a day, and every time it tells you: *Focus on me!*

Is it so strange, then, that it's hard to stop thinking about your phone while at school or at work? Is it strange that you must expend precious mental bandwidth not to pick it up? Is it strange that your phone is so alluring that you lose interest in your dinner company? Is it strange that you feel stressed—even panicked—when you lose the thing that offers up new experiences and rewards every ten minutes? Not really, is it?

CHAPTER 5

HOW DO SCREENS AFFECT OUR SLEEP AND MENTAL HEALTH?

It is surprising in a way that we don't suffer more mental illness than we do since we are in such an alien environment.

RICHARD DAWKINS, EVOLUTIONARY BIOLOGIST AND AUTHOR

SOMETIMES WHEN I'M ON the bus or train, I'll see someone who thinks they have lost their phone. They look as though they are suffering from severe anxiety, digging through bags and pockets as if their very life depended on it. And when they finally find it, the wave of calm that washes away their panic is clear to see. Of course, it's stressful to think you have lost something that cost hundreds of dollars, but maybe the anxiety attack isn't just about money.

When participants in a study were forced to give up their phones, their levels of the stress hormone cortisol began to rise after just ten minutes—in other words, the brain switched into fight-or-flight mode. The strongest effect was seen in people who used their phones extensively, while cortisol levels didn't appear to rise as much in people who only used them sporadically. This is not very surprising if you think about the way the brain has evolved.

It's important for our survival that we focus on the things that release dopamine. If something that gives us a small dopamine hit every ten minutes around the clock is removed, we'll react by becoming stressed, and the signal sent to the brain is that something beneficial to our survival has gone away. The HPA axis is activated and the brain yells at us: *Do something! Get back the thing that gives me dopamine! Now!* And it tries to make us do so by producing a strong sense of anxiety.

We feel stressed not only if we lose our phones but also if we use them too much.

Roughly 4,000 people in their twenties were asked to report on their cell phone habits and were then followed for a year. It turned out that those who used their phones a great deal had more problems with stress. In addition, they had more frequent symptoms of depression. The American Psychological Association came to a similar conclusion when they interviewed more than 3,500 people. The results were presented under the title "Stress in America" and showed that those who frequently picked up and looked at their cell phones were more stressed. Many seemed to realize that it might be wise to put their phone away from time to time, and two out of three agreed that a digital detox would probably be good for their well-being. Yet only a few—less than 30 percent—took action.

A review of several studies—a so-called meta-analysis—showed that there is indeed a link between stress and excessive cell phone use. The effect is minor to moderate, but for those with an increased vulnerability to stress, it may be the last straw.

What about anxiety—is the same true there? Yes, in nine out of ten studies, anxiety could be linked to excessive cell phone use. This comes as no surprise, since stress and anxiety activate the same system in the body—the HPA axis—but for different reasons. Stress is triggered by something that *is* a threat, anxiety by perceiving something as a possible but not certain threat. For example, if your boss yells at you, you may get stressed as the threat is here and now. But thinking that your boss may yell at you tomorrow is anxiety. If your phone is a driver of stress, it seems likely that it could also be a driver of anxiety—and that's exactly the case.

When study participants were asked to give up their phones and their distress and anxiety were measured, it turned out that their anxiety grew the longer they were separated from it. With each new test, every 30 minutes, their anxiety levels rose. And who were the most worried? Those who used their phones the most, of course.

Sleep is underrated

As we have seen, excessive cell phone use can lead to stress and anxiety—but the biggest impact is on our sleep. In recent years, in my work as a psychiatrist, I have noticed that more and more people are sleeping poorly and every other patient seems to be asking about sleeping pills. At first I thought it was a coincidence that so many of them came to see me, but that's not the case. The number of people seeking help for sleep problems has exploded, with almost one in three Europeans now reporting that they have trouble sleeping. We are sleeping less and less, averaging seven hours a night, which means that almost half of all Swedes sleep less than the seven to nine hours we need. The same pattern has been observed in many countries.

Several studies suggest that average sleep duration has declined by a whole hour during the last century! Looking even further back in time, our hunter-gatherer ancestors seem to have slept, if not more, then at least better. Research into tribes still living like our ancestors has shown that only 1–2 percent suffer from insomnia, compared to up to 30 percent in the industrialized world. In other words, modern man's sleep is in a sorry state.

DEPRESSED BY YOUR PHONE?

As you saw at the beginning of the book, prolonged stress increases the risk of depression. And as you have just read, our digital lifestyle and cell phones are drivers of stress. To this we can add another piece of the puzzle: the fact that one in eight Americans are now on antidepressants, the use of which has increased rapidly over the last decade. During the same period, stress-inducing smartphones have found their way into everyone's pockets.

It's not a stretch to suspect that our phones may have had something to do with it. So is there a risk that our phones are making us depressed? When researchers from Saudi Arabia studied more than a thousand people, they saw such a strong link between cell phone addiction and depression that they deemed it "alarming." In China, university students who used their cell phones a lot were found to be lonelier, less confident and more likely to be depressed. In Austria, depressed people were found to be more likely to use their phones excessively.

I could go on listing studies with similar results from other parts of the world, but I think you get the picture. Although it seems fairly obvious that cell phones increase the risk of depression, it could also be that depressed people use their phones more—rather than becoming depressed *by* them. It's therefore not possible to say that cell phones make us depressed.

Personally, I believe that excessive cell phone use should be viewed as one of several risk factors for depression. Not enough sleep, an overly sedentary lifestyle, social isolation and alcohol or drug abuse can also increase the risk of depression. Perhaps the most significant effect of our phones is that they take up so much of our time, we can't fit in the things that protect us against depression, such as exercise, socializing and sleeping well.

Why do we sleep?

We don't know for sure why we sleep, but it's safe to assume that the processes taking place in our brains and our bodies during sleep are extremely important. For our ancestors, spending one-third of one's life in a state where information from the senses is turned off must have come with great risks. In addition to the risk of being eaten, you were also of no use. A person who is asleep gathers no food and makes no offspring.

What's so important about sleep that nature has saddled us, and all other animals, with the need to do it? It's certainly not saving energy; the brain expends as much energy when we sleep as when we are awake. One reason is that, during sleep, the brain gets rid of waste products in the form of broken-down proteins that have accumulated during the day. In fact, this adds up to so many ounces per day that in a year's time the brain has cleaned out its own weight in "junk." This nightly cleaning seems to be important for the brain to function at all. The fact that long-term sleep deprivation increases the risk of a wide range of diseases—including stroke and dementia—is partly believed to be due to a disrupted "cleaning system."

Sleep deprivation also makes us function less well. Sleeping less than six hours a night for ten consecutive days impairs your concentration so much that it's equivalent to being awake for 24 hours straight! What's more, it affects our emotional stability. MRI brain scans of people being shown pictures of different facial expressions have revealed that the amygdala—the engine in our stress system—reacts more strongly if we haven't had a good night's sleep.

Yet perhaps the most important reason why we sleep is that, during the night, information is transferred from our short-term to our long-term memory through the process known as consolidation, which happens mainly during deep sleep. When we sleep, the brain chooses which of the day's events to store and turn into long-term memories. The brain can even re-create memories that are about to be lost during the night. If we don't get enough sleep, these processes don't work properly and our memory is disrupted.

Sleep is so important for the storage of our memories that it cannot be replaced. This was shown in a study of students who were asked to memorize a maze. Afterward, some were allowed an hour-long nap while the others stayed awake. Five hours later, they were tested to see how well they had learned to find their way through the maze. It turned out that those who had slept for a while remembered the maze better than those who had been awake, even though they had spent the same time thinking about the maze! In conclusion, it's not just practice that makes perfect, but specifically practice combined with a good night's sleep—something I find thought-provoking from an educational perspective, considering young people are sleeping worse and worse. You can read more about sleep problems among children and young people on page 80.

Stress—*and* screens—interfere with our sleep

But if sleep is so important for cleaning out the brain, for keeping us healthy and for our emotional stability, as well as for our memory and learning, why don't we fall asleep the second our head hits the pillow? Probably because it has historically been dangerous to sleep, as it means being completely cut off from all sensory impressions. When our hunter-gatherer ancestors went to sleep on the savannah, it was important that they were in a safe place where a predator could not sneak up upon them.

Therefore, we fall asleep slowly by gradually shutting down the impressions we get from our surroundings. This is probably why most people have trouble falling asleep if they get stressed before bed, as it activates the same parts of the brain—the HPA axis (see page 18)—that have historically been triggered by imminent danger. The brain's interpretation of this is that your location isn't safe enough and so it *should* be difficult to fall asleep. Your brain is still trying to protect you.

When you are stressed in the evening and can't fall asleep, your brain is in fact doing what it has evolved to do: keep you awake.

The dark side of blue light

Your circadian rhythm is partly governed by how much light you are exposed to. This process involves a hormone called melatonin, which tells the body when it's time to sleep. Melatonin is produced in a gland in the brain known as the pineal gland. Your melatonin levels are low during the day, rise in the evening and peak at night. When you are exposed to a lot of light, your melatonin production slows down and your body thinks it's daytime. That's why we sleep poorly if the room is too bright. If it's dark, however, our brains make more melatonin and the body thinks it's evening or night.

It's not just the amount of light we are exposed to that affects our melatonin production, but also the type of light. Blue light has a particular capacity to keep our melatonin production low. In our eyes are special cells that respond strongly to blue light—for our ancestors, it came from a cloudless sky—and these cells tell the brain to stop making melatonin: *Now it's daytime and you should be alert and attentive.* Simply put, blue light helped our ancestors to be active during the day and continues to keep us alert today.

When you use a phone or tablet before bed, the blue light wakes up your brain, not only suppressing the production of melatonin but even delaying it by two to three hours. Blue light thus turns back your biological circadian clock by several hours. Embellishing only a little, we might say that it creates jet lag equivalent to a trip to somewhere two or three hours from your current time zone. On top of this, cell phones tend to induce stress, and stress disrupts your sleep. As if this wasn't enough, your brain is kept awake by all the dopamine opportunities in the form of apps, social media and games that we discussed.

In theory, all this should make it harder to fall asleep if you use your phone at bedtime. But as we know, theory and practice don't always match up. So, does your phone really disrupt your sleep? Yes, it does. Researchers who studied more than 600 individuals can attest to this. The more time they spent on their cell phones and other screens, the worse they slept. They were particularly impacted if they used their phones late at night. Not only did they find it more difficult to fall asleep, their sleep quality also deteriorated. And of course, their risk of being tired the next day increased.

Just as your cell phone disrupts your concentration and memory just by being nearby, its mere presence in the bedroom seems to affect your sleep even when you are not using it. One study showed that children (aged 9–12) who kept their cell phones on their bed-side tables slept on average 21 minutes less than those who didn't. Having a TV in the bedroom can also be linked to a shorter night's sleep, but your phone is a bigger culprit. If 21 minutes doesn't sound so bad, there are studies that indicate an even greater impact. When parents were asked to estimate how long their children sleep, their assessment was that children who have a cell phone in their bedroom sleep an hour less than those who do not.

E-book vs. "regular" book

It's not just cell phones that are becoming more common in the bedroom—so are e-readers. In one experiment, a group of individuals were told to read a few pages from a book before falling asleep. Some read from a regular hard copy, while others read the same text as an e-book. The results? On average, the e-book readers stayed awake ten minutes longer than the hard copy readers—even though they had read the same text! But how is it different if you read a book on paper or on a screen?

To begin with, if you read an e-book on a tablet it affects both your melatonin production and the release of melatonin, which is delayed by around an hour. So, you might wonder, would all be fine if you just used a device with a paper-like screen? If I may speculate a bit, I don't think it is that simple. E-books are similar to cell phones. E-readers are therefore strongly associated with new information and activation of the brain's reward system, which we wake up just by holding them. When it comes to screens, the brain doesn't discriminate—and so we find it hard to unwind.

Some are more sensitive

There is, in other words, strong evidence to suggest that cell phones play an important role in the deteriorating sleep of both children and adults. At the same time, the sensitivity to stress and blue light from screens varies from one person to another. Some people fall asleep instantly despite exposing themselves to stress and screens just before bed. Others will lie awake because of anything the least bit stressful— just *looking* at their phones an hour before bed can be enough!

If you are a person who has trouble sleeping, try avoiding stress and screens late at night.

CAN SCREENS EVEN AFFECT YOUR APPETITE?

For people watching their weight, it's worth knowing that using your phone late at night can probably increase your appetite. Blue light not only affects the sleep hormone melatonin, it also increases levels of the stress hormone cortisol and the hunger hormone ghrelin. The latter not only increases your appetite but also makes your body better at storing fat.

In other words, blue light is particularly good at waking up the body (melatonin and cortisol), getting it ready to act (cortisol), replenishing its energy stores and making it store fat (ghrelin). After using a tablet or cell phone in the evening, you not only lie awake staring at the ceiling, you also feel a craving for food. As the icing on the cake, your body absorbs the calories in your late-night snack more efficiently, storing them around your waist in the form of subcutaneous fat.

In one study, researchers got to the bottom of how cell phones affect the brain's production of melatonin. Their advice—if you really must keep your phone in the bedroom—is to turn down the screen brightness before you go to sleep and hold it at least 14 inches away from your eyes. That way, your melatonin production won't be disrupted quite as badly.

As a psychiatrist, I am meeting more and more young people who ask for sleeping pills. My response is that before they even think about medication, they should leave their phone outside the bedroom and use an old-fashioned alarm clock. I also tell them to engage in physical activity regularly since numerous studies show that exercise both helps us fall asleep faster and leads to longer periods of deep sleep. Until this has been tried one should, in most cases, not consider sleeping pills. This might sound like the most obvious advice, but you would be surprised by how many of my patients come back and say it worked.

Chapter 6

SOCIAL MEDIA—OUR BIGGEST "INFLUENCER"

Comparison is the thief of joy.

**THEODORE ROOSEVELT, 26TH PRESIDENT
OF THE UNITED STATES**

IMAGINE THAT THE COMPANY you work for is hosting a conference. What do you think you and your colleagues will talk about in your free time? Your company's products, your competitors or the next quarterly report? Of course not. You will be talking about each other, because 80–90 percent of our conversations are about ourselves or gossip about others. We love to gossip! For many, the word "gossip" has negative connotations. But it doesn't deserve its bad reputation; gossip, too, has helped us survive. As you have seen, humans have historically lived in groups of 50–150 individuals and, naturally, some members of the group knew each other better than others. But even if you didn't have a close relationship with everyone, you had to keep track of the rest of the group. Gossiping is one very simple, very effective way of doing that.

We love to gossip

Being aware of what others are doing and their relationships to each other has historically been an advantage, so consequently we have a strong drive to acquire such information. Just as evolution has created a mechanism in our brains that rewards eating high-calorie foods with a sense of pleasure, thus encouraging us to eat them and avoid starvation, it has also built in mechanisms that provide a sense of pleasure when we acquire and disseminate information about others—that is, when we gossip. After all, both food and gossip have helped us survive.

Gossip not only provides information about others but also discourages antisocial behavior and attempts to take advantage of others. No one wants to be known as "the one who always disappears to the bathroom right as the bill comes." From this perspective, people who gossip might be seen as contributing to the well-being of the group.

Interestingly, we seem to be particularly entertained by negative gossip. You will probably be more interested to hear from a colleague that your boss embarrassed themselves by getting drunk at the conference than that they gave a good presentation. Negative gossip also strengthens our social bonds. When two people talk about a third person, it turns out that each feels a stronger connection to the other if they are saying something negative. In other words, you will feel closer to your colleague if the two of you talk about how your boss made a fool of themselves than if you discuss how good their presentation was.

But *why* does the brain prefer negative gossip? Probably because that information has been particularly important and taught us who we can trust and who we should keep at arm's length. For the same reason, we are particularly interested in conflict. If you have an enemy, it's valuable to know if there are others who share the same antagonist and could therefore be potential allies.

In a world where 10–20 percent of people were killed by another human being, information about who had an axe to grind with whom and who to watch out for may have been equally as important as information about where to find food. This is why, nowadays, televised election debates attract an audience of millions, while factual information about what each politician wants to achieve makes most people switch channels.

What about positive gossip, then—is it entirely useless from the brain's perspective? Far from it. Positive gossip makes us reflect more and inspires us to do better. Hearing about your boss's presentation will motivate you to deliver an equally good or even more impressive presentation yourself—even if it would have been *more* interesting to hear that they made a fool of themselves!

Social from cradle to grave

It's not only as protection against enemies that it has been important for us to keep track of each other through gossip. Unlike most animals, humans are deeply social, which has helped us cooperate and thus survive. The large number of studies showing that we live longer and stay healthier if we socialize—and risk getting sick and dying prematurely if we are too isolated—is one of the least surprising findings in the research.

Our social instincts are apparent even from birth. For instance, newborns focus more on lines that resemble faces than on random ones. In both children and adults, certain cells in the brain's temporal lobe process specific parts of faces. These cells work together in intricate networks to help you analyze the people you meet at lightning speed. In our time, our strong social urge to gossip, communicate and acquire information about each other has gradually moved onto our phones and computers. This drive has laid the foundation for one of the most successful companies of all time: Facebook, now known as Meta.

HOW MANY PEOPLE CAN YOU BE FRIENDS WITH?

The evolutionary psychologist Robin Dunbar at the University of Oxford has suggested that humans are capable of having relationships with about 150 other individuals. While we can recognize and remember the names of many more, the number of stable relationships—where we also know what a person thinks of others—is somewhere in that region. This is known as "Dunbar's number."

Interestingly, our hunter-gatherer ancestors are believed to have lived in groups of up to 150 individuals, and in primitive agricultural societies the average village size is thought to have been around 150 inhabitants. Dunbar believes it's the cerebral cortex—the outer layer of the brain and its most advanced part—that limits humans and animals in this particular respect. This means that the larger the cerebral cortex of a species, the bigger the groups they can belong to.

"The Facebook"

In February of 2004, 20-year-old Mark Zuckerberg launched a web-based social network called "The Facebook" for his Harvard classmates. It soon became clear that many more people wanted to join the network, which was then opened up to students from other universities and eventually to the general public. The interest seemed inexhaustible. Today, the number of people who have joined Facebook—which dropped the definite article from its name—is close to 3 billion.

One in three people on the planet is on Facebook—across every continent, almost every country and all age groups. *Everyone* uses Facebook. A lot. On average, we spend more than half an hour each day looking at each other's photos, reading updates and handing out or scoring likes. If we continue like this into the future, by the time today's 20-year-olds turn 80 they will have spent five years of their lives on social media, including almost three years on Facebook.

Almost three billion people use this product for more than half an hour a day—no other company in history has achieved anything like that before. Mark Zuckerberg has no doubt succeeded in capitalizing on our deep need to keep track of each other. But perhaps that's not the whole truth. In addition to the instinct to keep track of others, there is another human drive that has contributed to Facebook's enormous success: our desire to talk about ourselves.

We would rather talk about ourselves

A group of researchers wanted to find out what happens in the brain when we talk about ourselves. To this end, they gathered a group of test subjects to have their brains examined while they did precisely that. For example, they would share what they liked about skiing and might say: "Skiing is the best thing I know." Then they had to speculate on what someone else thought about skiing.

When the test subjects talked about themselves, the activity in parts of their brains increased compared to when they talked about someone else. These parts included the part of the frontal lobe behind the eyes known as the medial prefrontal cortex. This isn't surprising, as it's an area that's important to our subjective experiences. But the activity also increased in another area: the nucleus accumbens, commonly known as the brain's reward center. The same area that is activated by sex, food and socializing lights up when we talk about our favorite subject: ourselves.

There thus appears to be an inherent reward in getting to talk about yourself. Why is that? Well, the reason might be that by doing this we strengthen our social ties and improve our chances of cooperating with others. As an added bonus, we get an opportunity to see what other people think of us. When we notice how others react to what we say, we can choose to fine-tune our behavior. This inherent reward means that almost half of everything that comes out of our mouths in the form of speech is about our subjective experiences.

For almost all of human evolution, our audience was limited to one or a few people. But thanks to social media, we now have unimagined opportunities to tell our story to hundreds or even thousands of people. Though most people seem to like talking about themselves, we naturally differ in terms of just how much. The brain scans of the test subjects who were asked to talk about their own and others' experiences did show that activity in the reward center increased in everyone, but by different amounts. Interestingly, the biggest increase was seen in those who spent the most time on Facebook! The more our reward center is activated by talking about ourselves and receiving praise, the more active we are on social media.

(Anti)social media

With close to three billion users at your fingertips, social media is the optimal tool for keeping in touch with people. But are Facebook and other social media platforms really making us more social? Not necessarily. A study of nearly 2,000 Americans showed that those who used social media the most also felt lonelier than those who used it less. Whether they actually were more isolated is another matter; loneliness, as we know, cannot be quantified in terms of the number of friends a person has or how many text messages and phone calls they receive. It's something you experience. And that's precisely what seemed to be the case in this study.

Meeting online or in real life affects us in different ways. In one study, more than 5,000 people were asked questions about everything from their physical health to their quality of life, their general well-being and how they spent their time, including how much they went on Facebook. The results showed that the more time they spent on real relationships—that is, meeting people "in real life"—the better they felt. And the more time they spent on Facebook, the worse. "Social media makes us think that we are social and that we are doing something that is socially meaningful, but it is no substitute for real social interaction," the researchers concluded.

Loneliness cannot be quantified in terms of the number of friends a person has or how many text messages and phone calls they receive. It's something you experience.

WORSE AT SELF-CENSORING

If you have ever posted something on Facebook and later realized that you shared more than you originally intended to, you are hardly alone. Not only do we communicate with more people on social media, we also tell them more about ourselves because we can't see who we are talking to. Several studies have shown that we easily share details online that feel too personal to share face-to-face with another person. This is probably because we censor ourselves when we stand in front of someone else and see their facial expression and body language.

> *Wow, he looks a bit skeptical. I probably shouldn't say any more.* Without the possibility of feedback, we stop self-censoring. That's why we can share something personal with 300 people on Facebook that we wouldn't tell three people in real life.

But *why* did the people in this study feel lonelier and more downcast? Was it because they didn't have time to see their friends in real life when they were stuck in front of their screens? Another possibility is that they felt oppressed and isolated by being fed information about how happy everyone else is. Indeed, our place in the social hierarchy is an important factor in how social media affects our mental well-being. To understand why, let's look at another of the brain's messenger substances, which—like dopamine—affects how we feel: serotonin.

Serotonin is important for many mental processes. It is important for feeling calm and harmonious and having inner strength. It also appears to be important for how we perceive our status in a group. When researchers studied different groups of chlorocebus monkeys, they found that the alpha males had higher levels of serotonin—approximately twice as high as those of the less dominant monkeys in the group. This is believed to reflect the alpha male's perception of his own strong social position, his high self-esteem.

Serotonin seems to have a similar effect on us. In a study of university students at an American student dorm, researchers found that those who had been there for a long time and held leadership roles had higher levels of serotonin than those who had joined more recently. As a bit of a lark, they also measured the serotonin levels of the professor and their research assistant. (The levels were measured in the blood as they are difficult to measure in the brain.) The results? The professor had the highest serotonin levels!

A biological bridge between social status and well-being

Now, who is on top can change quickly in both monkey and human societies. In the monkey study, when for some reason an alpha male lost his position to a new male, his serotonin levels dropped sharply, while the new male's serotonin rose. Later, it proved possible to manipulate the power vacuum created when an alpha male was forced to step aside. When a random monkey was given an anti-depressant to increase his serotonin, he tended to take charge and became the new alpha. Interestingly, he created his new stronger social position by building alliances with other monkeys, not through physical intimidation.

Today serotonin is thought to influence a monkey's perception of its social status—and the same is likely true for us humans. It's probably not quite as simple as the one with the highest serotonin levels becomes the alpha. *Being* an alpha, and perceiving yourself to have a high social standing, seems to increase your serotonin, too.

In a cruel experiment, a pane of glass was placed between the alpha male and the other monkeys. The alpha could see them, but they could not see him. When he tried to influence the others with his gestures, they didn't care. As a result, he became frustrated and worried that he didn't have the same influence, and his serotonin levels dropped. The one in charge wants the world to know.

Interestingly, monkeys that had lost their alpha status not only had less serotonin but also changed their behavior, appearing tired, listless and depressed. Exactly why this happens isn't known, but one possible explanation is that the drop in serotonin—which contributes to social withdrawal—is nature's way of ensuring that the male who was forced to leave the position isn't a threat to the new alpha. Nature has developed a mechanism whereby the socially demoted male retreats and hides, so that he may return later when he has regained his strength.

In other words, this mechanism may be similar to what happens when we are stressed. In cases of severe and prolonged stress, the brain responds by lowering our mood so that we withdraw from a world it interprets as being full of dangers. If you are pushed out of your place in the hierarchy, the brain takes this as a sign to withdraw so as not to pose a threat to the person who has taken your place. The brain steers us toward this behavior through our feelings, with the result that we feel low and isolate ourselves.

I see the exact same pattern in real life, where as a psychiatrist I have treated thousands of people with depression. Over the years, it has occurred to me that cases of depression can be broadly divided into two groups: those caused by long-term stress, either at work or socially, and those caused by a loss of social status, such as being fired, being left by your partner or otherwise losing your social standing.

Digital envy

Like humans, chlorocebus monkeys have a clearly organized social hierarchy. For them, as for us, establishing one's place in the hierarchy is vital. That place has an important impact on how we feel, with serotonin forming part of the biological bridge between our place in the hierarchy and our well-being. It's easy to see that stepping down from a high position can be emotionally damaging—but let's stop and consider what this might mean. Competing against others and being in an unfavorable position, especially worsening one's position, seem to lead to anxiety and feeling low. Today all we do is compete. We compete in sports. We compete on our math test. On Facebook and Instagram, we compete to see who has been on the most exotic vacation, who has the most friends or who has decorated their bathroom with the most expensive tiles. And whatever the "game," someone always has us beat.

Haven't we always competed, though? Yes, it's true—but today the arena is very different from even 20 or 30 years ago. Growing up, I compared myself to my friends at school, and my role models were a set of rock stars as dubious as they were unattainable. Nowadays, children and young people are bombarded not only with pictures of their classmates, but also with photoshopped images of Instagram influencers setting an impossible standard for what is considered a good life. As a result, many feel they are at the bottom of the pecking order.

If we go back farther than my childhood in the 1980s, the differences are even greater. Our ancestors competed against members of their tribe, and in practice the competitors were probably no more than 20 or 30 individuals, since the others were either too old or too young. Today, we compete with millions of people. No matter what you do, there is always going to be someone smarter, better looking, richer or more successful than you. Thinking about this in the context of how our position in the social hierarchy can affect our well-being, it's not surprising that our newly connected world—in which we are constantly comparing ourselves to each other in every area—can affect how we feel.

One might suspect that the constant comparison that social media contributes to would undermine our self-esteem. And that's exactly what seems to be happening. When asked, two out of three Facebook and Twitter/X users stated that they felt inadequate. No matter what they did, it wasn't enough, as they were constantly being fed information that someone else was smarter or more successful than them. Not least in terms of their looks.

In a survey of 1,500 teenagers and young adults, 70 percent stated that Instagram contributed to making their body image more negative. In another survey aimed at 20-year-olds, almost half stated that social media made them feel unattractive. The same is true for teenagers. In one study, almost half of all respondents aged 12–16 said that they felt unhappy with their bodies after using social media. And girls' self-esteem seems to be eroded more than boys'.

Which came first, the chicken or the egg?

Anyone seeking to examine the effects of social media quickly runs up against the problem of which came first: the chicken or the egg? If we find that a frequent social media user is depressed, how do we know that social media is causing the depression? After all, it might just be that depressed people are drawn to Facebook and Instagram. Researchers tried to overcome this problem—known in scientific language as "causality"—by asking 20-year-olds to answer a few simple questions, including: "How are you feeling right now?," "How satisfied are you with life right now?" and "How much time have you spent on Facebook since we last asked?"

WHAT DO WE ENVY THE MOST?

When 600 people were asked about their overall feeling when using Facebook, the majority reported that it was positive. However, one-third experienced negative feelings. Most common was envy. What is it that makes us so envious on Facebook? Is it a new car or a freshly renovated apartment? Neither—it's other people's *experiences*. Vacation photos from exotic places make us more jealous than an expensive sofa or a fast sports car. And experiences are what we tend to share the most.

The questions were repeated five times a day and participants were asked to answer using their cell phones. They reported both how they were feeling at the time and how much they had been on Facebook in the last few hours. The results? The more time they had spent on Facebook, the less satisfied they were with their lives. If not proof, this is at least an indication that we may become less satisfied with our lives in the short term if we are bombarded with vacation or food pictures, each more exotic and exclusive than the last. The authors of the study summarized the results as follows:

On the surface, Facebook is an invaluable resource for fulfilling the basic human need for social contact.

But instead of improving our well-being, these results suggest that Facebook may worsen it.

The same phenomenon was observed by researchers at Yale University who measured the well-being of more than 5,000 people over two years. The more time they spent on social media in a given period, the worse their well-being in the months that followed. An even more important clue about how social media affects well-being came from Facebook themselves. In 2021, the *Wall Street Journal* released leaked internal documents that showed that Facebook's own researchers had warned senior management: "We make body image issues worse for one in three teen girls." The internal researchers—with access to data that external researchers could only dream of—warned that among British teens who reported suicidal thoughts, in 13 percent of the cases the desire to kill oneself came from using Instagram.

Facebook's management did not just ignore these warnings. They actively hid them from the public.

Social media affects us differently

You probably know several people who use Facebook a lot but still feel fine and don't seem to become isolated, depressed or jealous. Not *everyone's* well-being is negatively affected by spending a lot of time on social media. A number of studies have shown that it may make us feel worse, while others indicate that it can make us feel better—that people with many Facebook friends experience an increased sense of social support and well-being. Yes, even improved self-esteem! So what studies should we believe?

It's a good idea not to look at individual studies but to combine the results of several. A review of close to 70 different studies showed that social media has negative effects on our well-being, though the average effect is small. However, that's the *average*. Some groups are at an increased risk of being negatively affected by spending a lot of time on social media. One such group is people who are neurotic, constantly anxious and insecure. They are more negatively affected than those who don't have as many of these traits.

There are also ways of using social media that appear to be more strongly associated with negative feelings. Passive users, who only look at other people's photos and don't post their own or participate in discussions, seem to do worse than those who are more active. The latter not only post pictures but also communicate with others directly. It may sound obvious, but only 9 percent of all activity on Facebook involves active communication with others; mostly we are just scrolling through an endless feed of updates and photos. In other words, most people don't use social media to be social, but rather to check on what others are doing or as a platform to build their personal brand.

Those with a strong social support network outside social media use the latter as a complement to their social life and as a way of keeping in touch with friends and acquaintances. And many of them do feel a positive effect. On the other hand, those who use social media as a substitute for a social life feel worse. Studies have also shown that those who are already feeling down and have low self-esteem are at risk of feeling worse and having their confidence eroded even further by using social media too much.

A particularly vulnerable period

People who struggle with low self-esteem and insecurity are thus more likely to be negatively impacted by social media as they compare themselves to others more often. Is there a particular period in life when almost everyone feels insecure, anxiously comparing themselves to the people around them? Yes—adolescence. It's no exaggeration to say that today's teenagers are obsessed with social media. In a survey of 4,000 young people aged 12–16, one in seven (i.e., 14 percent) stated that they spent at least six hours a day on social media—more than one-third of their waking hours!

When, over a five-year period, nearly 10,000 children around the age of ten were asked how they felt and whether they were happy with their friends, looks, school and family, their overall well-being was found to decline over time. And it's not surprising, seeing as teenagers are generally more bored than younger children. One reason for this may be that the brain's dopamine system changes in adolescence. But interestingly, well-being fell particularly sharply among those who used social media extensively. This pattern was only observed in girls, however, who generally use social media more than boys. The researchers speculated as to what the connection might be:

Social media requires that they must always be available . . . They are constantly confronted with images of jammed in a door, the activity in your brain will be similar to the activity in the brain of the person whose finger got jammed. It's as though you can feel, if not the pain, then at least the discomfort.

Mirror neurons help us understand the pain of others by simulating it ourselves. And pain isn't the only thing we simulate. Mirror neurons also help us feel the joy, sadness and fear of others. They create a bridge between our outer and inner worlds, between other people and ourselves. Our innate drive to try to understand other people is called "theory of mind." Although mirror neurons play an important role, we don't fully understand how the brain goes about trying to understand what's going on in another person's head. What we do know, however, is that the brain takes in a lot of information when it makes its assessment. It picks up on not only what the person says, but also their eye movements, facial expression, body language, posture, tone of voice and how others respond to them. The brain processes all of this—often under the radar of our consciousness—and delivers the answer in the form of a perceived understanding of what someone is thinking and feeling and what their intentions are.

Theory of mind is always engaged as soon as you meet or see someone, and your brain is constantly trying to simulate what others are feeling. You might ask why. Presumably the aim is to help you understand what others will do and how you should relate to them. Remember that the brain is always trying to answer the question: *What should I do now?*

Our drive to try to understand other people's thoughts and feelings is probably innate, since mirror neurons are present in our brains from birth. But that doesn't mean we are born fully fledged masters of reading what's going on in other people's heads. It's a skill we must practice, and training starts early, during childhood and adolescence, when the most advanced part of the brain—the frontal lobe—gradually matures. How do we practice this?

By seeing our parents, siblings and friends face-to-face, we slowly build up a bank of experience that helps us make increasingly better judgments about other people's emotional states, thoughts and intentions.

For the mirror neurons in the brain to be as accurate as possible, we need to see other people—in real life. When researchers compared the activity in the mirror neurons when we socialize with others, as opposed to going to the theater or watching a film, it turned out that nothing activates our mirror neurons like meeting IRL (in real life). In second place came the theater. Films don't have the same effect; they do activate our mirror neurons, but probably not as intensely as when something is happening in the real world. In other words, if we watch something on a screen, big or small, it doesn't have the same effect as face-to-face communication on the biological mechanism that helps us create an intuitive understanding of the thoughts and feelings of others.

Is social media eroding our empathy?

Understanding what other people think and feel is the basis for one of our most important capacities: empathy. Empathy means being able to put yourself in someone else's shoes. It has been shown that the more abstract the person's suffering is, the more complicated it is for the brain, which normally has no problem understanding physical suffering. If you see a picture of someone with a broken leg, the areas of your brain that register pain are quickly activated—as though you were experiencing the pain yourself. If you find out that someone is suffering mentally, on the other hand, your brain will need more time. Relating to another person's depression or grief after a divorce is more difficult for the brain than understanding the pain of a broken bone.

Theory of mind is thus something we practice and that requires us to observe the facial expressions, movements and body language of others. What happens in a digital society when we replace personal interaction with text messages, tweets and memes? What happens when we isolate ourselves and socialize more through faceless communication, spending three or four hours a day staring at a screen? Does this make it harder for us to understand each other? And if empathy for *mental* suffering is particularly challenging for the brain, might our digital lifestyle make us less empathetic as adolescents, when our capacity for theory of mind is not yet fully developed?

Several scientists and intellectuals have warned that this is the case, including psychologists Jean Twenge and Keith Campbell, who have studied young people's behavior. They describe a "narcissism epidemic" unfurling in the wake of social media, as we increasingly focus on ourselves and ignore how others are doing.

This may sound speculative. Couldn't our digital world be making us *more* empathetic, since social media exposes us to people from all over the globe, broadening our horizons and giving us insight into other people's lives? Yes, that could be the case. But when some 70 studies were reviewed, the results indicated that Twenge and Campbell are on to something. The studies, which involved 14,000 college students, showed that they had become less empathetic since the 1980s. Two abilities in particular had deteriorated: the first, *empathic concern*, involves being able to feel compassion for those who experience hardship. The second, *interpersonal sensitivity*, means being able to take on another person's perspective and see the world through their eyes. And this hasn't just happened to college students; the same pattern is seen in secondary school students, who seem to have become more narcissistic since the late 1980s.

Might the increase be because the combination of cell phones and social media makes teenagers more egocentric and obsessed with status and appearance? *Mind your own business and don't care about others.* Is that why some people are more likely to pick up their phones to record an accident—in order to get a few likes on Facebook—than to help? The answer to these questions is that we don't yet know for sure. It's not possible to say with 100 percent certainty that our digital lifestyle is making us empathically numb, impairing our capacity for theory of mind. But we do know that there are a number of worrying signs.

Who owns your attention?

Have you ever asked yourself why you bought the clothes you are wearing? Was it because they looked good or because the price was right? At some point, you have been told about those particular items of clothing, and the same goes for most of the things you own. Someone has told you that your phone, your furniture, your TV and your computer are available to buy and convinced you that you need them.

According to the consultancy firm McKinsey, the global advertising market has an annual turnover of more than a trillion dollars. It has rapidly moved from newspaper, TV and street ads into the phones in our pockets—a development that isn't the least bit surprising given the way our brains work. As you have seen, securing our attention is the first step in creating long-term memories, and it is thus an important condition for our perception of commercial messages. After all, we have to remember what it is we want! You have also learned that social information is important and something we remember because it has helped us survive.

Digital marketers exploit this. They know that your attention is glued to a gadget that gives your brain hundreds of tiny dopamine hits every day. They know that your thirst for information about the people around you makes your brain ready to store new information. They are also aware that your brain will create positive associations—both conscious and subconscious—with the message they want to feed you. All they have to do is ingeniously place their ads in your social media feeds.

Your phone's ability to feed you commercial messages is simply unparalleled. And not just because of its capacity to grab your attention, but also because of the possibility to sneak in messages precisely where they will have the most impact. You have probably seen ads in your Facebook and Instagram feeds that are so cleverly placed they are hard to distinguish from your friends' posts. The placement is tailored to present you with the message when your emotional state makes you the most receptive. Someone who has just looked at Facebook photos from a soccer game is a suitable candidate for sporting event ads, while someone liking a vacation shot may be interested in booking airline tickets.

The most valuable thing today is not money, Bitcoin or even gold—it's your attention. For a marketer, it's hard to think of a better tool to grab your attention than your phone. And in your phone, it's hard to imagine a more effective way to target messages than through social media. That's how, in the span of 15 years, Facebook went from being a dorm-room project to completely taking over the world's advertising market. They won the battle for your attention and blew the treasure chest wide open. Today, Meta is worth more than half of Sweden's gross domestic product. As the company presents its interim reports, stock investors closely examine how long users stay on Facebook. Every minute is precious and brings new opportunities to sell ad space. The company is therefore incentivized to try to keep users on the site for as long as possible.

A digital arms race

The aims of most car manufacturers are to make cars better, safer, more environmentally friendly and cheaper. Any car company that doesn't measure up to this will sooner or later go bankrupt. For Facebook, Snapchat, TikTok, and other social media platforms, their biggest asset is your attention, so they constantly need to create products that are better at attracting it—otherwise they too will go bankrupt. The competition for this hard currency—your attention—is getting fiercer by the day, in a digital arms race in which companies making apps, phones, games and social media platforms are using increasingly sophisticated mechanisms to cut through the noise. In order to grab your attention, they are getting better and better at hacking your brain's dopamine system.

Look at the apps on your phone. The colors are bright and the symbols simple and effective. The phone looks almost like a slot machine. And that's no coincidence—behavioral scientists have carefully studied which colors the eye is drawn to. Social media apps such as TikTok and Instagram have tried to mimic slot machines by making you swipe down on your screen to see new photos and messages, and it takes them a few seconds to appear—like pulling on a one-armed bandit and hoping for three cherries! The consequence? Your brain's love of unknown outcomes kicks in.

Twitter has its own version. When you launch the mobile app, the white bird pulsates a few times against a blue background before growing so large that it fills the screen—suddenly revealing the tweets. This is not because it takes time to log in or because your connection is unstable, but because Twitter is building suspense by making you wait. The duration of the delay has been carefully calibrated to maximally trigger your brain's reward system. It's also no coincidence that push notifications often use the same sounds as text messages. This makes you think that one of your friends has sent you a message—hacking your brain's need for social interaction—when in fact it could be someone trying to sell you something.

Meta, Snapchat, TikTok and Twitter's products are not platforms that allow you to freely share messages, images and digital validation—their product is your attention, and they capture it *using* messages, images and digital validation in order to sell it to various advertisers. If you think you are getting something for free, you are sorely mistaken.

"perfect" bodies or "perfect" lives, which makes it difficult not to compare oneself with others.

There is thus a lot to indicate that social media can make some teenagers and adults feel low and isolated and maybe even erode their self-esteem—and it seems to be worse for girls. But perhaps the effects are even more far-reaching.

We see ourselves in others

Some 30 years ago, a group of Italian scientists wanted to understand what happens in the brain when we make certain movements, so they studied a group of monkeys. When the monkeys reached for food, cells in what is known as the premotor cortex—an area of the brain that helps us plan our movements—were activated. The strange thing was that when they saw other monkeys reaching for food, the same cells were activated. The cells that the researchers had discovered are not only found in monkeys but also in humans and are known as mirror neurons.

Mirror neurons are brain cells that help us learn by imitating others. These neurons are thought to be the reason why, if you stick your tongue out at a newborn baby, it responds by doing the same. But mirror neurons are not only important for learning motor skills; they are found in many areas of the brain. One of these areas—the somatosensory cortex—helps us understand what other people are feeling. When you see a picture of a person getting their finger

Technology should adapt to us

If there is so much money to be made from our attention, in the future will we have phones and social media platforms that are even *better* at capturing it? In a few years' time will we be spending seven or eight hours a day in front of our screens, completely replacing our social contacts with digital facsimiles? Or will we have phones, tablets, computers and apps that help us manage new technologies better? It's actually up to us. As soon as we demand it, we will see phones and social media platforms that work in better harmony with the human brain. The day we stop buying iPhones and logging onto Facebook because they make us feel or function worse, Apple and Meta will be forced to create new products. But it's naïve to think that this will happen spontaneously.

Some argue that it's pointless to worry about how technology is designed. *It is what it is, get used to it.* But I think that's wrong. Technology isn't something we have to accept regardless of how we feel about it. Technology should adapt to us, not the other way around. Phones and social media platforms are ingeniously designed to be as addictive as possible. They *could* have been designed differently— and they still can. If we decide that we want other products, we will have them.

When I see people in the street who are so engrossed in their phones that they seem oblivious to what's going on around them, I often think: *Is he controlling his phone or is his phone controlling him?* I'm not alone in thinking this way; representatives from several of Silicon Valley's tech giants—especially those who work with social media—have expressed remorse over their products. Chamath Palihapitiya, a former senior executive at Facebook, said in an interview that he feels guilty about what social media is doing to us: "The short-term dopamine-driven feedback loops that we have created are destroying how society works." Sean Parker, a former Facebook board member, notes that the company has exploited a vulnerability in human psychology. Parker doesn't mince his words either: "God only knows what it's doing to our children's brains."

A violent history of "us and them"

As you saw at the beginning of the book, our ancestors lived in a dangerous world where starvation, infections, accidents and predators were so common that half of all people died before the age of ten. Yet perhaps the greatest threat came not from lions, infectious diseases or starvation but from other people. We have been extremely cruel to each other. A surprising number of excavated skeletons have an injury on the left side of the skull, probably from a blow to the head by a right-handed person.

Among hunter-gatherers, 10–15 percent are believed to have been killed by another human being. And we have good reason to believe that things got even worse in primitive agricultural communities, with up to one in five people beaten to death (the increase is believed to come from more resources to fight over in agricultural societies compared to hunter-gatherer societies).

And these are murder statistics *within* the tribe; *between* tribes it was likely even worse. Leaving your own tribe and going in search of other *Homo sapiens* effectively meant heading to your death. So what relevance do these dismal figures have in today's society? Well, they form the basis of one of the most important social drives in human beings: dividing each other into "us and them." It's the expression of a fear of the unfamiliar and especially of those who look different to us. As it turns out, the amygdala reacts immediately to people we don't recognize.

Seventy thousand years ago there were 100,000–200,000 of our species in East Africa. A small portion of them left the continent, perhaps as few as 3,000 individuals. These people—no more than would fit in a modern shopping center—are believed to be the ancestors of all the people on earth living outside Africa today. If our origins can be traced to such a small group, it should mean that we are genetically similar. And that's precisely the case. Humans are more homogeneous than almost any other species: between two people, 99.9 percent of our genome is identical. Yet we *look* so different!

The truth is that our external differences are mainly adaptations to the climate. For example, our skin color is related to the amount of ultraviolet radiation we are exposed to. Because fair skin is better at converting vitamin D into its active form, those of us living in sun-deprived parts of the world have developed pale skin. There are also genetic differences in how well we tolerate cold temperatures. The shape of Asian people's eyes, with a fatty skin fold, is believed to be a legacy from their Mongolian ancestors living in the freezing cold.

The minor genetic differences between people in different parts of the world today are largely skin deep and an adaptation to the environment in which their ancestors have lived. Below the surface, we are surprisingly similar. Yet our innate fear of anything foreign has led us to make a big deal out of these external variations. The amygdala would rather signal danger one time too often than one time too few—the smoke detector principle!—and will tell us to watch out when we see a stranger, especially if they happen to look different.

If asked whether I'm prejudiced, I would like to say no. But like many others, I'm more prejudiced than I think. The brain is exceptionally quick to draw conclusions based on what we see, without us even being aware of it. Of course, this doesn't mean that we should heed our dark urges and, for example, behave in a racist way. However, it's important to know about this innate mechanism, as this evolutionary remnant from a bygone era can influence us on a subconscious level. The fear of that which is—and those who are—different is perfectly logical if we consider the bloody history of mankind, but today it makes no sense at all.

Alternative facts and fake news

On the internet, our strong urge to divide people into us and them, along with our innate fear of danger and disaster, have a very tangible effect. Today, more people get their news from Facebook than from newspapers and TV, and there is an important difference between these sources. Newspaper editors and television newsrooms choose which news to present, evaluating both whether a story is interesting and whether it's true. The news in our Facebook feeds, on the other hand, is selected by a computer program—an algorithm. Meta has no editorial team responsible for ensuring the truth value of what's written in the articles that get shared. The algorithm selects the news it *thinks* we will be interested in—that is, what our friends have read and shared. Whether the news is true or not doesn't matter.

Since 10–20 percent of people throughout history have been beaten to death, we are particularly interested in news about conflict and threats. That kind of information has been vital. If you want to get someone's attention, tell them about a conflict. As Facebook's algorithm crassly bases its selection on how likely we are to read and share the news, one might suspect that stories related to conflict and threats would spread particularly quickly. The same goes for very positive news—regardless of whether it's outright lies.

And that's precisely what appears to be the case. When researchers studied how more than 100,000 news stories spread on social media, they found that fake news not only spread to more people, but it also spread faster. It took six times longer for a true news story to reach as many people as a fake one. The reason seems to be that fake news is more sensational—by definition, it doesn't have to stick to the truth—and since we are therefore more likely to read it, the algorithm prioritizes it, placing it at the top of our feeds. Moreover, our tendency to share fake news means it's not just the algorithm's fault that it spreads. The algorithm makes sure it reaches us, and then we do the work of passing it on to our friends. The more people who read and share it, the more familiar and true we believe it to be.

Facebook, the largest news source in human history, has been criticized for not taking editorial responsibility for the accuracy of the information it disseminates. Critics say that the company is exploiting our innate fears and interest in conflict to attract our attention—and sell ads. Fake news on social media has fueled military conflicts, helped spread conspiracy theories on an unprecedented scale and influenced the outcome of democratic elections. And the information we see is all decided by the algorithms that have discovered patterns in what we focus on and exploited them.

Time for a digital detox?

If social media is making us stressed, causing envy and spreading fake news, it's probably not a bad idea to cut down on your

"Facebooking." When nearly 150 American university students were asked a series of questions about how they were feeling, as expected the results varied: some felt fine, others were suffering from mild depression. By random selection, the students were divided into two groups. One continued to use social media as normal, while the other was only allowed to spend a maximum of 30 minutes a day on Facebook, Instagram and Snapchat combined—ten minutes on each platform.

Three weeks later, those who had cut down their social media time to just 30 minutes a day were doing better, and those who'd had symptoms of depression at the start of the study felt less depressed and isolated. This suggests that social media *can* in fact make us depressed, not that depressed people use social media more. The point of the study, however, is that participants didn't have to quit social media entirely; they felt better simply from limiting their time. No one knows for sure how much you need to limit your social media usage in order to avoid negative effects—the choice of 30 minutes in the study was arbitrary.

Those who would consider not just cutting back on social media but actually taking a break or giving it up entirely would probably see an even greater effect. In Denmark, nearly 1,000 people tried this for a week and, as a result, they felt more satisfied with life, less stressed and spent more time face-to-face with other people. The experiment also showed that different people see different effects. The positive effect was particularly palpable for those who experienced a lot of envy from being on Facebook, and also for those who were passive users and only read other people's posts without leaving any comments. But none of this is likely to surprise you after reading this chapter.

CHAPTER 7

WHAT ARE SCREENS DOING TO CHILDREN AND YOUNG PEOPLE?

We limit how much technology our kids use at home.

STEVE JOBS, FOUNDER OF APPLE

IN 2022, A MAJOR SURVEY of Swedish online habits was presented, "Swedes and the Internet," and surely no one was surprised that it showed we are obsessed with our phones. Yet there was one finding that made almost everyone gasp, and that's just how big a role we have come to let the digital world play in our children's lives—even the lives of very young children. The survey found that one in four babies—i.e., those 0–12 months old—are entertained with the internet, and more than half of all two-year-olds are shown it *every day*.

When it came to school-age children, the percentage of kids

who were online climbed further. A clear majority of seven-year-olds use the internet daily and virtually all eleven-year-olds (98 percent) have their own cell phone. Swedish teenagers spend seven hours a day on their phones, tablets, computers or in front of the TV. If you discount the time they spend eating, sleeping and traveling to school, this leaves only 10–12 hours in a day—a staggering two-thirds of that time is spent in front of a screen.

Sweden is not unique, of course. A similar British survey showed that children and teenagers in the UK spend more than seven hours per day using screens. (In the mid-1990s, that figure was three hours.) According to another study, American teenagers spend nine hours a day online. And similar figures are pouring in from around the world. For adults, there seems to be a mental price to pay for spending too much time in front of screens. So how bad is it for children and young people? That's what we'll take a look at next.

Cell phone addiction in children

"How was your vacation?" I ask a friend who has just returned from a week on Mallorca with her family. "Well . . . the weather was amazing and the hotel was nice, but it wasn't exactly a success," she replies, telling me it's been a week full of conflict—and *all* the conflicts were about the children's screen habits. When they refused to put their phones and tablets down at the dinner table, discussion and quarreling ensued, ending with the parents forcing them to leave their devices in another room. Still, the children were fully focused on the vibrating updates from their phones, which they could hear through the thin hotel walls. "What's even the point of all that fussing and fighting when they were equally uninvolved anyway? The pull of their phones was just as strong from the other room," she says glumly.

The brain is made up of various parts and systems that work in parallel and sometimes even against each other. When you stand in front of a bowl of chips at a party, one system in your brain will tell you to wolf down every last crumb, while another will pump the brakes, reminding you both of the upcoming swimsuit season and not to embarrass yourself. These systems develop during different stages of life. We know that the frontal lobe—the part of the brain that sits behind the forehead and helps us resist impulses or postpone rewards—matures last. It's not fully developed until 25–30 years of age. The part of the brain that tells you not to eat all the chips is pretty subdued in children and teenagers, while the parts that push you to go ahead are anything but quiet at that age.

As you saw in the previous chapter, cell phones have an extraordinary ability to activate the human reward system and thus attract our attention. The part of the brain that slows our impulses not only helps us resist the bowl of chips, it also helps us resist the urge to pick up our phones. The fact that it's underdeveloped in children and young people makes our digital technologies even more irresistible to them. You have seen the consequences: children staring at their phones in restaurants. At school. On the bus. On the sofa. Scenes where children scream and cry when their phones are taken away from them. Constant arguments and fights.

Dopamine in different parts of life

In the previous chapter, you read that dopamine motivates us to do different things. When we talk about dopamine levels, what we really mean is the level of activity in the brain's dopamine system—i.e., both the amount of dopamine that is released and how many receptors it can dock with on the surface of the brain cells.

The activity in the dopamine system decreases over the course of our life, with an estimated decline of about 10 percent per decade. But that doesn't mean we feel unhappier with age—quite the opposite. What it does mean is that we don't experience the same highs as we get older and aren't prepared to take the same risks. Dopamine activity peaks in adolescence, when levels rise as sharply in the case of a reward as they fall with disappointment. This means that both the highs and the lows are bigger and can make teenagers feel particularly alive and euphoric. At the same time, going through something like a break-up can trigger enormous sadness.

The combination of a not yet fully developed system for impulse control and the ability to feel higher highs means that young people often take big risks. It's no coincidence insurance companies often refuse to insure 18-year-old motorcyclists or that skydiving clubs won't train 15-year-olds. Another consequence is that young people are at increased risk of addiction. This is an important reason for being extra restrictive about introducing alcohol early in life. Phones, on the other hand, we don't seem the least bit afraid of introducing, despite their formidable capacity to activate the brain's reward system. Studies of how frequently people of different ages use their phones can roughly be summarized to conclude that the younger you are, the more time you spend on your phone. Teenagers use cell phones more than adults, and younger teenagers use them the most.

Mobile learning isn't for young children

In an early childhood memory, I'm sitting glued to the TV in our living room, trying to count on my fingers with the help of *Fem myror är fler än fyra elefanter* (*Five Ants Are More Than Four Elephants*). This Swedish cult kids' show is an educational masterpiece that helped many in my generation to learn how to count and write. Plus, it was highly entertaining!

There is no doubt that TV shows like *Five Ants* can help children learn numbers and words and even develop reading comprehension, but there is much to suggest that children need to be quite close to school age to benefit from educational TV programs. For young children, such as two- or three-year-olds, the benefits seem less significant, and they probably learn more from interacting directly with their parents or other people.

It's entirely possible that apps on tablets and phones can have the same positive effects as *Five Ants*, though there hasn't been much research into that yet. But from a learning perspective, children approaching school age seem to benefit more, as with educational TV shows. When iPads and tablets are placed in the hands of two-year-olds and called "learning tablets," there appears to be a great deal of wishful thinking involved.

Hugo Lagercrantz is professor emeritus of pediatrics at the Karolinska Institute in Stockholm, Sweden, and has devoted his entire professional life to understanding the brain's development in children. He is critical of the idea that tablets could speed up children's development and argues that there is in fact evidence to suggest they *slow down* the development of young children in particular. He believes that many misconceptions about the usefulness of technology for very young children stem from thinking of them as "tiny adults." Let's take jigsaw puzzles as an example. For an adult, there might not be much difference between doing a puzzle in an app or in real life. However, a two-year-old doing a real-life puzzle is training their motor skills and thus developing a sense for different shapes and materials. This is lost when playing on an iPad.

Another example is the ability to write by hand. There might seem to be little point in bothering with cursive when everyone types on a keyboard anyway. *Let's throw out all those old notebooks from the classroom and focus on tablets and computers instead!* Sure, that might work for adults who already know how to write, but if you haven't mastered written language, learning to write with a pen can help you recognize the letters. In preschool children, studies have shown that the motor skills involved in writing by hand—i.e., with pencil and paper—are closely linked to the ability to read.

WHY DOES THE FRONTAL LOBE MATURE LAST?

The brain matures from back to front. The part at the back of our neck matures first and the frontal lobe behind our forehead last. Why is it that the frontal lobe—the impulse-controlling part of the brain—takes so long to develop? One reason might be that the frontal lobe is also important for social interaction, which is extremely complex in humans. We need several decades to practice and gain experience, and it makes sense that the part of the brain that needs lengthy training matures last. This also means that this part of the brain is probably influenced more by our environment than by our genes.

In order for us to understand and participate in complex social interactions, our frontal lobe needs training, which some researchers believe may be jeopardized by our digital lifestyle. When we spend a large chunk of our social lives in front of screens instead of meeting face-to-face, the frontal lobe doesn't get the social skills training it needs. For most people, this probably doesn't make much difference, but for those who have difficulty judging other people's thoughts, feelings and intentions from the outset—for example, people with autism—a lack of social training may have consequences.

There is a group of American pediatricians who share Lagercrantz's concerns. In the journal *Pediatrics*, they warn that children who spend too much time on tablets and phones instead of playing are not developing important motor skills, which they will need in order to learn math and theoretical subjects later on.

Lagercrantz and the American pediatricians have on their side the American Academy of Pediatrics, which recommends that children's access to tablets and cell phones be restricted, especially if they are younger than 18 months. To me, "younger than 18 months" sounds completely absurd, since children of that age can't even talk properly and some can barely walk! However, I quickly realized that the recommendation isn't the least bit absurd in view of the fact that 80 percent of all two-year-olds are actually exposed to the internet on a regular basis.

In an article titled "Let Kids Play," the American Academy of Pediatrics pointed out that children's brains need play in order to develop impulse control, the ability to focus their attention and social functioning. The problem is that children don't play anymore. "We're in a climate where parents are feeling like they need to schedule every minute of structured time, and . . . play is seen as irrelevant and old-fashioned," they note, recommending that doctors prescribe play to stressed-out parents so that they can find the time to fit it into their own and their children's busy schedules.

Worse at postponing rewards

We all wrestle with dilemmas like *If I don't eat the whole bowl of candy, I'll be in better shape for the summer* or *If I stay home and study instead of partying, I'll land a better job.* The ability to forgo an immediate reward in favor of an even greater one in the future is incredibly important. How good children are at this can actually indicate how their lives will turn out later.

This has been interpreted to mean that our capacity for self-control is both expressed early and important for our possibilities in life. But the ability to postpone a reward isn't just something we are born with; it's also influenced by how we live and can be trained. So how does our digital lifestyle affect this ability? Several studies have shown that people who use their phones a lot are more impulsive and find it more difficult to postpone a reward. But couldn't it be that impulsive people use their phones more?

In an attempt to settle the eternal question of which came first, the chicken or the egg, a few years ago a group of researchers decided to put smartphones in the hands of individuals who didn't already have one. (Today it's virtually impossible to find a single person who doesn't have a phone.) What they wanted to test was whether the ability to postpone a reward was affected by using a cell phone. And indeed, after three months of using a smartphone, a series of tests revealed that the participants had a harder time postponing rewards.

If you can't postpone a reward, you may not be able to learn things that it takes time to get good at. One sign of this may be that the number of students learning to play an instrument has dropped sharply. When asked why this might be, one music teacher said that children today are so used to instant rewards that they give up when they aren't immediately good at something.

Cell phones at school—friend or foe?

A couple of weeks after my book *Hjärnstark* (*The Mind-Body Method*) was first published in Swedish, I received an email from a principal asking if I would consider giving a lecture at her secondary school. During the lecture in the school auditorium, I estimated that about half the students looked down at their phones at some point. Disheartened, I concluded that I must have been boring to listen to. "Not at all, on the contrary. It's been a long time since I've seen them this engaged," the principal said encouragingly. "But half of them were fiddling with their phones?" I objected. "Well, yes, but you should see what it's like in the classroom. There, they are *all* on their phones and the teachers struggle enormously to get their attention. At an elementary school where I used to work, the students didn't even go out and play at breaktime. They just sat with their phones."

On the way home, I thought about what she had said about the students fiddling with their phones in class. My history teacher would never have accepted me bringing a Game Boy to school! Nor would my math teacher have looked the other way had I brought a portable TV to watch a film. And if, against all odds, my teachers had allowed Game Boys and TVs in the classroom, how on earth would I have been able to learn anything?

Today many schools have banned cell phones in class. Personally, I think that should be a given, but it remains a controversial issue. So what does the science say about the impact on children who bring their cell phones to school? To begin with, children write more if they don't have their phones in the classroom. When American researchers observed a number of children in the same class, those who didn't have their phones took more notes—a lot more notes. They also learned more. When asked about the lesson afterward, they remembered more than those who had their phones with them.

Perhaps there is a point to reading on paper, too. Researchers in Norway instructed half of a group of secondary school students to read a short story on paper, while the other half read it on a tablet. It turned out that those who read the short story on paper remembered it better—even though everyone had read the same text. What they remembered in particular was the order in which things happened in the story. One possible explanation is that, on a digital tablet, the brain is used to receiving constant dopamine rewards, in the form of emails, text messages and status updates. This forces the brain to spend important bandwidth ignoring the tablet instead of fully concentrating on the text, with the result that we learn less. How much better is paper for reading comprehension? According to a 2018 study on children aged 9–12, reading from paper instead of from a screen improved reading comprehension by no less than two whole years, which means that a sixth grader reading from a screen has the same reading comprehension skills as a fourth grader reading on paper.

A distraction—for some

Since these studies strongly suggest that you learn more by both writing by hand and reading on physical paper, it seems obvious that tablets and phones should be kept outside the classroom. However, we should always be careful when interpreting individual studies. It is always better to look at the pooled results of many. When a group of researchers reviewed more than a hundred different studies, all on how cell phones affect learning, they could hardly have been clearer in their conclusion: "Multitasking with cell phones distracts learning via different ways and mechanisms." In other words, cell phones disrupt learning in both children and adults. At the same time, the researchers were careful to point out that some individuals are more affected than others.

Although there have been more than a hundred experiments on this, a clear majority of which show that cell phones disrupt learning, these kinds of studies can feel abstract and contrived. Psychological tests trying to determine how children or adults learn by arbitrarily assigning them to different groups seem far from reality. So what would really happen if cell phones were removed from the classroom?

In the UK, cell phones were banned in a number of schools across London, Manchester, Birmingham and Leicester. Students were asked to hand them in in the morning and got them back at the end of the school day. Consequently, their results improved. The scientists behind the study estimate that the phone ban resulted in sophomores learning so much more that it was equivalent to an extra week of school per academic year! And struggling students improved their results the most. The conclusion was that a cell phone ban is a cheap way to level educational differences among students.

It is also worth noting, though, that high achievers may actually benefit from keeping their phones, or at least be less held back by them. But for others, they're nothing but a distraction. This fits well with the findings in a review of the experiments above: students were affected to different degrees. When the memory, concentration and language skills of more than 4,000 children aged 8–11 were tested, those who spent less than two hours a day in front of a screen performed better. However, other factors beside their phones also played a part. Those who slept 9–11 hours a night had better results, as did those who were physically active.

It's not possible to say exactly what effect limiting screen time had and how much came from sleeping well or being physically active. Indirectly, cell phones may also affect how much we sleep and how physically active we are, as they tend to disrupt our sleep and make us more sedentary. The researchers' conclusion is simple: for children to function as well as possible, they need to be active for at least an hour a day, sleep between 9 and 11 hours and use their phones for no more than two. These recommendations for sleep, activity and screen time are hardly an impossible ideal, but how many children actually meet them? I'll tell you: 5 percent.

The erosion of young people's sleep

As you have seen, more and more of us are having problems sleeping, especially young people. Teenagers having trouble sleeping may be nothing new; during adolescence we undergo a shift in our circadian rhythm. Entering our teens, we become more of an "evening person" and struggle to get up in the morning. At the same time, a teenager needs nine to ten hours of sleep—considerably more than an adult. A large need for sleep combined with an out-of-sync circadian rhythm makes it difficult to get up in the morning. For this reason, some researchers have suggested that the start of the school day should be delayed for secondary school students, to bring it more in line with their biological circadian rhythm.

Even though teenagers have always slept more or less poorly, their issues have worsened in the last decade. Among 15–19-year-olds, the proportion diagnosed with a sleep disorder has increased by an unfathomable 700 percent since 2007. Although these issues had been on the rise even before 2007, the change was slow and at comparatively low levels. But that was the year when the number of people seeking help for sleep disorders began to rise sharply, and in 2011 it went into overdrive. In other words, the pattern is the same as for people seeking help for mental health problems. And you know what happened in 2011: smartphones really took off and the iPhone went from being a luxury product that only a few could afford to finding its way into the pockets of just about everyone, including children and young people.

The amount of sleep young people are getting is decreasing even faster than in adults. A study of the sleep habits of nearly 700,000 children across 20 countries found that they sleep less today than they did ten years ago—a development that, ironically, has taken place during a period when we have been inundated with new research on the importance of sleep for young people. So how much less do they sleep, according to the study? A whole hour compared to ten years ago! In other words, it's not too wild to guess that the stressful lives of teenagers—with nearly 3,000 cell phone swipes a day keeping them awake at night—have contributed to the trouble many of them have sleeping.

But at the risk of sounding like a broken record, can we really know that phones are the reason they are sleeping poorly? In Norway, 10,000 teenagers were asked how much sleep they felt they needed and how much they actually got. They also reported how much time they spent on tablets, phones and computers or watching TV. The results showed exactly the same pattern as for adults: the more time spent in front of a screen, the more trouble sleeping. We can't be 100 percent certain of the causality, but it is very likely that cell phones are a major contributor to poor sleep among young people.

In the UK, half of all children and young people between the ages of 11 and 18 reported checking their phones at some point during the night. One in ten do it *at least* ten (!) times. And they weren't exactly naïve about the consequences—almost 70 percent said that it affected their schoolwork. The rise in sleep problems is particularly evident in girls, and one possible explanation might be that they spend more time on social media than boys, who are more likely to play games. In order not to miss out, girls feel a need to be available and connected at all times. The constant dopamine hits this produces—combined with the stress of always being present and comparing themselves to others—makes sleeping particularly difficult.

The kids are not OK

I'm glad I'm not a teenager today. This selfish thought strikes me when I read that the number of teenagers being prescribed anti-depressants increased by 130 percent in Sweden between 2012 and 2022. Anxiety and depression are on the rise and young women are hit hardest—one in nine girls and women aged 15–24 are prescribed antidepressants. Sweden is by no means an exception. In the UK, a staggering one-third of all teenagers report having been prescribed antidepressants, and in 2023 the US Centers for Disease Control and Prevention reported that 57 percent of teenage girls feel persistently sad or hopeless and nearly one in three teenage girls have seriously contemplated suicide. These figures indicate that teenage sadness and suicidal thoughts have increased 60 percent during the last decade.

What has caused this? The short answer is that we can't be certain but it is likely that our digital lifestyle has contributed. Since the 1990s, one study has tracked the lifestyle of American teenagers by each year asking a large group how they spend their time: whether it's hanging out with friends, dating, drinking alcohol, sitting in front of a screen, studying or playing sports—anything that might be part of a teenager's life. The questions also cover how they feel—whether they are sad or anxious—and how they sleep.

Even though it's difficult to interpret the responses to such surveys, in recent years a pattern has emerged. The more teenagers sit in front of screens, the more they struggle with feeling low. Those who spend upwards of ten hours a week in front of a screen report being the least happy. They are followed by the group that spends between six and nine hours, who in turn are less happy than those who report spending four to five. And so on. Everything associated with screen time—social media, browsing, watching YouTube videos and playing computer games—was linked to poorer well-being. Doing other things, however—such as socializing and playing sports or an instrument—was associated with improved well-being.

This pattern recurs in other studies. A review of 16 surveys involving more than 125,000 children and young people showed that more than two hours of screen time per day increases the risk of depression. The more hours, the greater the risk. When 40,000 children and young people were surveyed, diagnoses such as depression and anxiety were found to be twice as common among those who used screens for more than seven hours a day, compared to those who were more frugal with screen time.

Seven hours a day sounds like an absurd amount of screen time. Blocking out time for sleeping, commuting, school and eating, we are left with no more than eight or nine hours in the day. How common is it for teenagers to spend almost all of that time on their phones? Turns out it's not uncommon; seven hours is actually the average daily amount of screen time for teenagers in the US, and 6.5 hours is the average in the UK.

It's not just in Europe and the US that researchers have made this connection. In China, data from almost 130,000 children and young people were examined, and the more time they spent in front of a screen, the higher their risk of depression. The risk increased most strikingly among those who used screens more than two hours a day. However, there are studies showing that limited screen time can have a positive impact on our well-being. In those cases, it's a matter of one or two hours a day—far from the six to seven hours that young people are spending in front of screens today.

Can cell phones make young people depressed?

So we can say for sure that cell phones are behind the deterioration of young people's well-being? Not so fast. Perhaps sad and anxious adolescents simply spend more time in front of screens. Back to the eternal dilemma of the chicken and the egg! To shed light on this issue, a group of researchers decided to study the effects of cell phone use on the risk of depression and anxiety over time. Four thousand young adults were asked to complete a questionnaire on two occasions, one year apart. The responses showed that those who reported using their phones a lot at the time of the first questionnaire were at an increased risk of sleep disorders, depression and stress in the period that followed. This suggests that cell phones contribute to depression and sleep disorders and that it's not just those who are sad, stressed and sleeping poorly who use their phones more.

The study also found that screen time was more closely linked to mental health problems in teenagers than in children. One explanation might be that teenagers use social media, while children play games and watch films. As you have seen before, we are affected by social media because constantly comparing ourselves to others results in stress that can make some people feel down. In 2022, a major UK study was presented with similar results. Over the course of a year, researchers followed 17,000 children and teenagers. The subjects were regularly asked how they felt and how much they used their phones and social media. It turned out that social media usage actually had a negative effect on their well-being, but only for girls between 11 and 13 and for boys between 13 and 15. This corresponds to the period of puberty. One possible explanation is that we are particularly vulnerable to comparing ourselves to others during puberty, and too much exposure of others' "perfect" facades on social media creates feeling of inadequacy.

Another way to make headway in the chicken-or-egg dilemma is by looking at how trends in the data have changed over a long period of time. The psychology professor Jean Twenge, who has studied teenage behavior, noticed that something happened around the year 2012—something so dramatic that she had never seen anything like it, despite studying data going back to the 1930s.

In 2011, American youth began to feel lonelier and sleep worse. They no longer spent as much time with their friends and stopped dating, drank less alcohol and weren't interested in getting a driver's license. That same year, the iPhone went from being an exclusive luxury gadget to selling more than 120 million devices annually. Almost as many iPhones were sold in 2011 as between 2007 and 2011. Suddenly, the majority of young people owned a smartphone.

Though the studies you have just read about might lead you to think that cell phones are contributing to more young people seeking help because they are feeling low, when I read them, I couldn't shake a sense of alarmism. Maybe this is all just a manifestation of that same old moral panic I saw when my parents' generation was horrified by music videos and hard rock. Maybe, I thought, cell phones have nothing to do with it. It's probably all due to changes in society—with, for example, increased demands on those entering the job market. The stress of this manifests as young people pushing themselves harder and harder in school, making them feel lonely and unwell.

But then I started looking closer at that argument. Most evidence suggests that teenagers spend no more time on homework today than they did in the 1980s. And those who do dedicate a lot of time to schoolwork seem to be feeling better than those who don't. Changes in the education system with unclear goals and less priority placed on reading may have contributed to young people's ill health in some countries, but school systems have hardly changed in the same way and at the same time across the world. The trend toward increased mental illness among young people, however, has been observed in a large number of countries.

Yet couldn't it all be due to a bleaker job market following the 2008 financial crisis, which made it harder for young people to find work, leading to anxiety and poorer well-being? Of course, this may have contributed. But the labor market and the economy have been impacted before without the same dramatic change in our well-being. What's more, the number of young people seeking psychiatric care has increased across all social groups, regardless of whether they come from affluent or economically disadvantaged homes. And the same trend is observed across all ages. For example, the proportion of 12–14-year-olds seeking psychiatric care has risen sharply—and at that age, your chances of entering the job market aren't usually your top concern.

Then it occurred to me that mental illness has gone from being a taboo subject to, nowadays, something people speak more openly about. Could this be the reason why a growing number of people are seeking help? Sure, but why would the numbers rise so sharply during this period in particular? More people talking about mental illness and finding the courage to seek help has been a gradual development over many years. And the same reasons for hiding your problems don't apply to anonymous surveys, where young people have been indicating that they are feeling worse and worse.

When broadband went mobile

The biggest change in young people's lives during the period 2010–2016, when many more people started seeking help for mental illness, was that mobile broadband went from being virtually non-existent to claiming an average of four hours of our time every day. Such a massive, rapid change in the behavior of young people—or adults, for that matter—has never happened before in modern times. Chances are, there has never been such a rapid change of lifestyle ever in human history.

As you read earlier, there are several possible mechanisms by which excessive cell phone use can cause mental illness in young people, both by creating stress that makes them feel unwell and by making them feel "less than." Constantly comparing yourself to others and having your every move scrutinized by hundreds of peers through Facebook and Instagram can make you feel like you are at the bottom of the social hierarchy.

An even more important way that excessive cell phone use can impair young people's well-being is by taking time away from other things that protect against mental illness. When children and young people spend six to seven hours in front of a screen every day, they don't have time for play and "real" social interaction. They also don't have time to be physically active or get enough sleep. For most people, it may not matter much, but for those who have increased vulnerability to mental illness and are heavy users of their phones and social media, it can be the straw that breaks the camel's back. To summarize, the most important impact of digitalization on our mood and well-being might not be what we do online but what we *don't* do when we are online. What gets crowded out.

Well-being vs. addiction

One way to find out what effect something has is to see what happens if you take it away. These types of studies are difficult to carry out in the case of cell phones, however. When researchers gathered a thousand students from ten different countries to study how being without their phones for a day would affect them, more than half called off the experiment. They simply could not spend a day without their phones.

Those who made it through the phone-free day were asked to write down their experience. One student from Chile was all but traumatized, a British student was amazed that he had managed it at all and a Chinese student said he was "unable to express my feelings without media." Not everyone's experience was quite so nightmarish, however. "I interacted more than usual with my surroundings," one student noted. Another described it as "one of the best days I have had with the people I live with."

Many teenagers seem to realize that they have lost control over how much they use their cell phones. In Denmark, almost half of all surveyed secondary students felt they were using their phones too much. The same pattern was observed in the US, where 50 percent of young people felt they had become addicted. Among girls, the proportion was even higher: around 60 percent. That girls in particular seem to have more problems with sleep, well-being and cell phone addiction is a pattern seen in survey after survey. But is it an exaggeration to call it an "addiction," like one American youth did? Perhaps they were simply adding color to express themselves.

Addiction means repeatedly exposing yourself to something

despite knowing that doing so is harmful. Let's clarify what that means in the case of cell phones. In this case, "repeatedly" is undeniably true, given that teenagers and adults alike pick up their phones every ten minutes, every waking hour. Can it be deemed "harmful" if doing this risks ruining your sleep as well as your ability to concentrate, and if you spend a couple of hours each day on something that, in retrospect, you usually find quite pointless? When you could be studying, hanging out with friends, playing sports, reading a book or practicing an instrument instead? Consider instead whether *you* deem it that harmful. In that case, you might call it an addiction.

Personally, I think we *can* speak of "cell phone addiction." That doesn't mean, of course, that phones are "digital heroin" or that they turn children into "psychotic junkies," as one American doctor argued in an opinion piece. Such wild exaggerations risk downplaying the addictive effects of cell phones. Naturally, something can be addictive without being on a level with heroin. However, someone who doesn't shy away from comparing phones to drugs is Chris Anderson, the former editor-in-chief of the tech magazine *Wired*. "On the scale between candy and crack cocaine, it's closer to crack cocaine," Anderson says.

The concept of screen time

Screen time is far too broad a concept. It's one thing to talk to your cousins on FaceTime or look up facts for an essay on Wikipedia and it's another to play Candy Crush Saga or scroll mindlessly on Facebook. There are many great examples of how both young people and adults can gain knowledge and skills using digital technologies.

Computer games can improve our spatial awareness and train us to solve problems. Pilots and surgeons in training learn to handle critical situations in the cockpit or operating room through advanced simulation programs. Such positive examples also exist for children.

Torkel Klingberg, professor of cognitive neuroscience at the Karolinska Institute, has shown that both children and adults can train their working memory with the help of computer games. The method improves concentration and can even reduce ADHD symptoms. The autism researcher Simon Baron-Cohen has developed software to help autistic children understand the feelings of others through films that put faces on cars and trains. It takes advantage of the children's interest in such objects to help them practice interpreting facial expressions.

In the previous chapter, you read that we have a natural drive to both discover and learn new things—a drive so strong that it's sometimes difficult to distinguish between reward-seeking and information-seeking behavior. With the help of digital tools, this drive can be harnessed to help us learn everything from mathematics to languages, history to science. In other words, it's important not to hit the panic button just because something involves a screen. At the same time, it's naïve to think that our use of screens will self-regulate. It's unrealistic to put a cell phone in the hands of a seven-year-old and expect them to be able to handle it; it is simply too addictive, and we have never evolved a defense mechanism. It's like putting a bag of candy and a stack of comic books on your child's desk and telling them to only have *one* piece if they are *really* hungry and to only read the magazines when they need a short break. For some students this might work, but most will struggle.

CHAPTER 8

EXERCISE—A SMART ANTIDOTE

The brain is organized for movement. If we don't understand that then we are going to miss much.

MICHAEL GAZZANIGA, PROFESSOR OF PSYCHOLOGY AT THE UNIVERSITY OF CALIFORNIA

When I get home from work, I'm totally exhausted. My whole body is crying out for some downtime on the couch, but I know that the best way to unwind is to lace up my running shoes and head out for a run. When I get back, the stress is gone—I feel better, calmer and more focused. I wish I had realized this earlier in life.

A 46-YEAR-OLD PROPERTY DEVELOPER tells me how he manages his stress and anxiety with physical activity. I have heard hundreds of versions of this story from people in hospital consulting rooms, in the street and in letters and emails describing the positive effects of exercise on their well-being. But the fact is that the impact of physical activity on how we feel is only the beginning—virtually all our mental faculties work better if we exercise. It improves our concentration, memory and stress tolerance.

In a time when many people feel stressed, distracted and overwhelmed by a flood of digital information, physical activity is a smart antidote. Perhaps the best there is.

The information tsunami

Every day, 3.2 quintillion bytes of data are created. A quintillion is a billion billion! Such a big number is impossible to grasp. Perhaps it's easier to absorb that, every minute, 240 million emails and 16 million text messages are sent. In that same minute, 500 hours of material are uploaded to YouTube. In addition, 2.4 million Google searches are made and 350,000 tweets are posted, while 1 million pictures are swiped either left or right on Tinder. And every day, we are speeding up. Yet the brain tasked with handling this flood of digital information is the same as it was 10,000 years ago.

To manage the flow of information, we need to be able to resist our own impulses—both the impulse to pick up our cell phone every few minutes and the impulse to click on the link that will take us away from the article we are reading. There is a psychological test known as the Stroop test that measures this very ability. In the test, the name of one color is displayed in letters of another color—like the word "yellow" written in red letters, for example. The task is to state the color of the letters as quickly as possible and avoid saying the color that's written on the screen. This may sound trivial, but under time pressure it's actually quite hard. (Try it yourself—Stroop tests are available online.) Although the test is simple, the results actually give a good indication of your ability to suppress different impulses.

When adult test subjects are physically active for 20 minutes before taking a Stroop test, they perform better—much better—and have an easier time resisting impulses. The effects are noticeable after a single walk or run, but the ideal is to be physically active on a regular basis for several months. Children, too, find it easier to resist impulses after physical activity, which has been put into practice in several Swedish schools. While the format has varied, typically the children engage in physical activity in groups for 15–20 minutes before the start of the school day, so as not to steal time from other subjects. These initiatives have been organized by enthusiasts—such as teachers, principals or parents—who want to put the research findings into practice.

The results of the initiatives have not yet been compiled in any research report, but two articles, one in the Swedish newspaper *Göteborgsposten* and one on Sweden Television's news site, with the headlines THEIR GRADES ARE RISING WITH THEIR PULSE and

PULSE TRAINING BEFORE SCHOOL—STUDENTS IN BODEN HAVE RAISED THEIR GRADES, indicate that their efforts are bearing fruit. The children are learning more and becoming calmer with physical movement, and many have reported that they are better able to concentrate and less impulsive. But getting 15–20 minutes of movement into your day before school isn't easy, given the sleep needs and circadian rhythm of children and young people. One might thus be curious whether interventions even shorter than 15 minutes are effective. Turns out, they are.

Even a little movement pays off

When more than 100 fifth graders were physically active every day for four weeks and underwent a series of psychological tests both before and after the experiment, they became not only more focused but also better at directing their attention. They were even able to process information faster! The truly fascinating revelation was how *little* physical activity was needed. The activity took place in the classroom and lasted for six (!) minutes a day. The students took a short break from their regular classes and watched a video with movements that they were asked to imitate to practice their coordination. The movements got progressively more difficult but were still a far cry from complicated soccer drills and jumps over a vault. And six minutes a day is such a short time that it hardly interferes with the regular curriculum.

This daily six-minute program lasted four weeks, but just doing it once had an effect! When a group of children and young people were asked to play the computer game *Prince of Persia*, which contains a number of demanding puzzles, they performed better if they got some movement in before starting the game. And once again, it wasn't a matter of long movement sessions—by running for just *five minutes*, they were able to play better. One of the struggles for children today is concentrating and avoiding distraction, yet they got better at doing just that after only five minutes of physical activity. Interestingly, the ability to concentrate improved even more in children with ADHD—a diagnosis based on having severe difficulties concentrating.

Can teenagers and adults improve their focus, too? Yes, actually, they can. When 300 teenagers wore pedometers for a week, it turned out that the more they moved, the better their concentration—especially if they got their heart rate up. A review of some 30 different studies of both teenagers and adults came to the same conclusion: exercise has a positive impact on the major scarcity of our time—concentration. The review also showed that physical activity improves executive functions such as our abilities to plan and shift focus. Teenagers' ability to concentrate improves after a single walk or run, while the effects on their executive functions require regular physical activity over a number of weeks or months.

Why do we focus better?

The answer is probably that when our ancestors were physically active, like when they were hunting or being hunted, they needed their concentration the most. Over millions of years, evolution has honed our brains to enable us to focus when we truly need to—which was likely when we were hunting or fleeing. Hunting may seem like a rare activity, but studies of modern-day hunter-gatherers suggest that our ancestors spent between two and three hours a day hunting and doing other work. During those hours when we were moving about, we had to pay maximum attention, which a person who managed to catch what they were hunting (or avoided becoming a snack for the thing hunting them) probably did!

Exercise is a way of "hacking" evolution.

Because the brain has remained largely unchanged since our days on the savannah, our concentration also improves when we are physically active. But you and I don't need our focus for hunting or avoiding predators, we need it to sit still at our school desks or to give a presentation at work. Exercise then becomes a way of "hacking" evolution and using a biological survival mechanism to function optimally in our time. This is exactly what's happening in a number of schools today, with very promising results!

Exercise prevents stress in both children and adults

Having met hundreds of people who have used physical exercise to improve their functioning and strengthen their brains, I have found that it's not the effect on their concentration that people value the most, it's the effect on their stress and anxiety levels.

As you saw earlier in the book, one in *eight* adults have been prescribed antidepressants in the US. Even though antidepressants are used to treat both depression and severe anxiety, I personally think that number is too high. Though medications are very useful, they are sometimes prescribed a little too liberally. And yet there are people who should be taking antidepressants but aren't, despite having major problems with anxiety. For them, physical exercise can be a real miracle cure.

A set of university students, all of whom were highly sensitive to anxiety, were divided into two groups: one was prescribed high-intensity exercise (20 minutes of running at 60–90 percent of their maximum heart rate) and the other low-intensity exercise (20 minutes of walking). The activity took place three times a week over a period of two weeks—i.e., six sessions in total. Hardly an insurmountable training regimen. After these six sessions, both groups had reduced their anxiety levels, but the effect was particularly pronounced among the runners. And their anxiety levels didn't just drop immediately after the sessions but throughout the 24 hours following. The effects lasted even longer than that. A full week after the training program had ended, their anxiety levels were still lower.

According to the World Health Organization, 284 million people struggle with an anxiety disorder. But as numerous studies show, anxiety isn't as common among those who are physically active. When 15 studies involving nearly 700 patients were reviewed, the results showed that exercise and training protected against anxiety regardless of whether they were diagnosed with an anxiety disorder or just had anxiety within the "normal" range. And like in previous studies, those who got their heart rate up saw the biggest impact.

Mental airbag against stress

When I explain to my patients who struggle with stress and anxiety that physical exercise can reduce their symptoms, many are surprised.

"Shouldn't relaxation have that effect?" they ask. For the vast majority of our time on earth, stress has largely been linked to dangers that you either have to fight or flee from. Whether you choose to attack or take to your heels, you will have a better chance of survival if you are in good physical shape. If you are, you don't have to rev up your stress system quite as much and can outrun a threat without needing to throw your body into "panic mode."

Because the stress system has remained unchanged since our days on the savannah, those who are physically fit are better not only at escaping lions but also at coping with the stressors of modern society. When an accountant who goes running regularly doesn't get as stressed as her colleagues during tax season, the biological reason is that her stress system evolved during a time when stress meant running away from predators. Thanks to her good physique, she doesn't have to put as much strain on her stress system when going through quarterly reports and giving presentations.

Anxiety, as you already know, is the process of activating the stress system in advance of something that *might* become a threat— the smoke detector principle. The same evolutionary logic applies here: a fit person doesn't need to activate their stress system in advance because they are better equipped to attack or outrun a potential threat. This results in less anxiety.

The evolutionary logic that physical exercise makes us more stress and anxiety resistant because stress has been a signal of the kinds of dangers that a fit person is better equipped to handle may sound reasonable. But a theory being reasonable doesn't carry much weight in science. Therefore, let's say that you are hearing a sound at a certain volume coming toward you, starting from 15 feet away.

Then you hear the exact same sound played in the same place 15 feet away, but the source of the sound is now moving away from you. The sounds should be perceived as identical—they are the same tone, played at the same volume and in the same location—but the strange thing is that you will perceive the sound coming toward you as louder and closer.

The reason why your perception of the sound doesn't match reality—known in scientific language as "cognitive bias"—is probably that sounds coming toward you could be dangerous and a safety margin is needed to avoid them. To make us alert to potential approaching dangers, evolution has built in a margin of safety that makes us perceive sounds coming toward us as louder. A study shows that people in good physical shape perceive the two sounds as the same, whether the source of the sound is coming toward or moving away from them. This is believed to be because those who are in good shape don't need a head start. They can more easily outrun what is approaching and so the auditory impression doesn't need to be distorted.

That we perceive sounds coming toward us differently depending on our physical fitness is a strong indication that, historically, those who have been in good shape haven't had to put as much strain on their stress system. This is the evolutionary logic behind the stress-preventing effects of physical exercise.

We move our bodies less and less

So, we know that physical exercise boosts our stress tolerance and helps us manage our digital environment by giving us more of the great scarcity of our time—concentration. The problem is that we are moving our bodies less and less. Studies of tribes still living as hunter-gatherers in primitive agricultural communities show that our ancestors probably took around 14,000–18,000 steps a day. Today, we take fewer than 6,000 steps per day—and every decade, that number is dropping. The average fitness level among Swedes has fallen by 11 percent since the 1990s and almost half of all adults are now so unfit that it poses a direct health risk. It's particularly bad for young people. Physical activity among 14-year-olds has fallen by 24 percent for girls and 30 percent for boys since the turn of the millennium. Such a rapid decline can hardly have occurred before in human history. What is the main reason for the drop in physical activity among 14-year-olds? Screen time. There is no reason whatsoever to think that this alarming trend has been any different for most Western countries.

How much exercise do we need?

In what way and for how long should adults and children be active in order to make their brains work better? To answer that question, a group of Israeli scientists reviewed close to 5,000 research studies—now that is quite the undertaking!—all of which explored the effects of physical activity on our mental faculties. Of the most well-designed studies, they selected just under 100. And what did they conclude? That *any* type of physical activity is good for our mental faculties. Walking, yoga, running or strength training—*all* have a positive effect. The faculty that improved the most with physical exercise was our mental processing speed. Physical activity quite literally makes you think faster.

WE ARE IN TERRIBLE SHAPE!

Imagine meeting one of your forefathers or foremothers—your great-great-great-grandfather if you are a man; your great-great-great-grandmother if you are a woman. Go back so many generations that the person in question lived 10,000 years ago. Probably one of your first impressions of this temporally distant relative would be how fit they are. You see, we are in worse physical shape than our ancestors—*much* worse.

An analysis of thigh bones and tibias/fibulas/shinbones/ calf bones that are more than 7,000 years old showed that, back then, the *average* bone quality, mass and strength were on a par with those of today's long-distance runners. The physique of the most athletic hunter-gatherers exceeded that of today's top athletes. The Cambridge scientist Colin Shaw describes our ancestors as "monsters" in terms of their fitness. "Even our most highly trained athletes pale in comparison to these ancestors of ours. We're certainly weaker than we used to be," says Shaw.

Shaw believes that the main cause of the gradual deterioration in our bone quality is reduced physical activity. As our lifestyle has gotten increasingly sedentary, our bones have become more porous and our bone strength has decreased. In other words, it's not only the brain but also the body that is at risk of functioning less well in our increasingly sedentary world.

The ideal would be to move your body for at least 52 hours over a six-month period, which equates to two hours a week—for example, divided into three 40-minute sessions. More than that doesn't really seem to have any additional effect on the brain, except of course that you will improve your physical fitness. From the brain's perspective, the effect seems to wear off somewhere after two hours a week, so you don't need to run a marathon to see positive results!

For the brain, it's good get your heart rate up. That said, you will get surprisingly far simply by walking at a brisk pace. Do what you can—and if you get your pulse racing, it's an added bonus.

CHAPTER 9

THE FUTURE BRAIN— WILL IT ADAPT?

The silicon chip will transform everything,
except everything that matters.

BERNARD LEVIN, *THE TIMES*, OCTOBER 3, 1978

IN THIS BOOK, you have read about the negative effects of cell phones on our mental faculties, like memory and concentration, and also how our modern, more sedentary, lower-sleep lifestyle has the same consequences. Does that mean we are getting dumber? *Wait a minute*, you might be thinking, *haven't we gotten smarter?* While that's true, it's only in the long term.

The average IQ in the Western world has increased by 30 points in a hundred years. The first modern IQ tests were developed in the early twentieth century, and the average score was—then, as now—100 points. As we have gotten smarter, the tests have had to be made more difficult. A person taking an IQ test today and scoring 100 points—that is, the average—would have scored 130 on the test used a century ago and would thus have been in the top 3 percent of the population. Similarly, someone who scored 100 points in the early twentieth century—and was classed as being of normal intelligence at the time—would only get 70 points on today's test and would basically meet the criteria for an intellectual disability.

However, people who lived a hundred years ago were no dumber than we are. They handled practical aspects of life at least as well as we do. The likely explanation for our rising IQ is that modern man has gotten much more training in the kind of abstract and mathematical thinking measured by an intelligence test. For example, almost 85 percent of all European adults have completed secondary school education, compared to a hundred years ago, when most only got seven years of primary education. Today's jobs are more complicated. Let's take my own as an example: a hundred years ago, medical doctors didn't have many drugs to choose from; antibiotics hadn't even been discovered at the time. Today, there are thousands of medications available and our medical knowledge is so extensive that no one can know everything.

Our IQ is falling

As we have moved into an increasingly complex world with more complex jobs and longer education, we have developed our mental faculties and practiced the skills measured by an IQ test. That each generation gets a higher IQ is known as the Flynn effect, after the New Zealand professor James Flynn. But it's not true that the Flynn effect is caused only by digitization. The increase in our IQ has been more or less steady since the 1920s, and back then there was no television or internet.

Since the late 1990s, however, Flynn has observed a worrying pattern: in Scandinavia, the increase has slowed and the average IQ is now falling slightly each year. Not very dramatically—the drop is only 0.2 points per year—but over a generation it could fall by 6–7 points across the Scandinavian countries. That's far from insignificant. Perhaps, Flynn speculates, the rest of the world will follow suit.

Flynn, who passed away in 2020, was not sure what was causing this trend but speculated that this may be because school isn't as demanding and doesn't prioritize reading in the same way it did 20 or 30 years ago. Another contributing factor could be that we are getting less and less exercise. And a further reason might be that we are struggling to deal with all the information flooding over us.

"The Knowledge"

When I take a cab in London, I'm always amazed that the driver can find their way around without a map or a GPS, even though the street system is not only big and sprawling but also seems to lack any kind of structure or logic. It's no coincidence that this is where I have been lucky enough to land a particularly experienced driver—becoming a cab driver in London is a big challenge and you must be able to memorize more than 20,000 streets and 50,000 locations. The knowledge bank that prospective drivers must acquire is so extensive that it's referred to as "the Knowledge." Although many spend years preparing, half of them fail.

The learning process is so extensive that it even creates measurable changes in the brain! When researchers compared prospective cab drivers training for Knowledge tests with their regular peers, there were no differences in their brains before the learning period. However, when the scan was repeated afterward, they found that the brain's memory center—the hippocampus—had become larger in those who had passed the test! In particular, the part of the hippocampus that is closest to the back of your head (known as the posterior hippocampus) had grown, which is important for our ability to orient ourselves spatially. In contrast, in their peers and those who had failed the test, the size of the hippocampus remained unchanged.

The hippocampus growing and becoming physically larger in response to learning is an example of the brain being changeable, or *plastic*. We are now beginning to understand why the hippocampus of prospective cab drivers grows as they learn the streets of London. Driving without a GPS in an unfamiliar environment activates both the hippocampus—which is important for memory and locating yourself spatially—and the frontal lobe—which is involved in decision-making. In situations where we are faced with multiple choices, such as a three-way junction, these areas in particular light up. When we follow a GPS, on the other hand—receiving instructions such as "in 100 feet, turn left" or "at the roundabout, take the first exit"—the hippocampus and the frontal lobe aren't activated in the same way. Earlier in the book you read that the brain likes to save energy and therefore won't put effort into something it doesn't need. Thus there is a risk that if we don't use certain mental faculties, we might lose them.

For the brain, the general rule is: use it or lose it.

As we delegate more and more tasks to our phones and computers, we might therefore suspect that we are gradually losing other mental functions than just navigation. But maybe we are freeing up mental capacity that we can use for something else? If you have a GPS that's helping you find your way, you can focus instead on listening to a podcast or thinking about a work problem. Well, maybe. But we can't outsource *everything*. We need some knowledge to be able to relate to the world, ask critical questions and evaluate information—especially in an age that's becoming more and more complicated. An increasingly complex society makes us smarter—the Flynn effect—but also seems likely to dumb us down if we leave too much of our thinking to computers and phones. This may have contributed to the trend of declining IQ that we are seeing in Scandinavia.

Many jobs will disappear as a result of automation and artificial intelligence. Those that are left will probably require us to concentrate. Ironically, focus is both the thing we need most in a digital world and the thing that such a world erodes.

"Railway madness" and other fears

"[The] modern world with an overabundance of data is both confusing and harmful to the mind"—the prominent Swiss scientist and polymath Conrad Gessner warned early of the negative impacts of modern technology. Very early. He wasn't referring to cell phones or the internet but to the printing press, and his warning was issued in the mid-sixteenth century. During the expansion of the railway in the nineteenth century, there were doomsday prophets who warned of a "railway madness." Traveling at speeds beyond 20 miles per hour was so unnatural, they said, it would result in nausea, mental anguish and even trigger violent outbursts! A few decades later, it was the telephone that was considered the devil's invention, attracting thunderstorms and evil spirits. These fears were so widespread that telephone companies sometimes struggled to recruit operators to work the switchboards. In the 1950s, people feared that TV sets were having a hypnotic effect!

Perhaps our fears of how our digital lifestyle might affect the brain are the equivalent of railway madness, haunted phones or being hypnotized by the TV. It's the same knee-jerk complaints from the doomsayers ahead of every new technological change! That is, of course, possible, but there is a case to be made for taking our current concerns seriously. Unlike before, we now carry our new technologies with us everywhere we go and interact with them virtually around the clock. Nobody sat on a train for six to seven hours a day. No one talked on the phone for six hours daily or carried a TV around in their pocket. The fact that we use cell phones and computers more or less constantly is what sets the situation apart from previous technological revolutions.

The brain is an organ that never ceases to amaze with its ability to adapt to the world around us. Given this malleability—the brain's plasticity—it would almost be strange if our 24/7 digital lifestyle didn't have a powerful effect on us.

Science can't keep up!

There are new studies coming out every day on the effects of our digital lifestyle, and it's easy to feel like your head is spinning with all the new findings. However, one thing is important to remember: research takes time. Four or five years often go by from the time researchers begin to plan a study to when they have recruited participants, conducted the experiment, analyzed the results and compiled them in a scientific journal. This means that the planning for many of the studies that are being published today began as early as 2018–2019, and since then the time we have been spending on digital media has risen sharply.

In other words, digital developments are outpacing the research into their effects. If you want to know what science has to say about today's digital lifestyle, you will have to wait until 2027. Of course, our technologies will have developed even further by then, and unless the trend of the last 25 years is suddenly reversed, we will be using cell phones and computers even more. Should you wish to know how our digital lifestyle in 2027 will affect us, you will have to wait until 2031.

My point is to urge caution. If you have to rip your children's cell phones and tablets out of their hands—or your own—you might suspect that the technology is addictive. If you find yourself sleeping poorly and becoming more anxious or distracted while spending three hours a day on your phone, it might be worth putting it away for a while—regardless of what the research has shown so far.

What do we lose along the way?

As you saw earlier in the book, humans have a natural tendency to be easily distracted—a tendency that our phones seem almost purposely designed to hack. "But if we are being distracted by Facebook instead of a lion, aren't we just returning to our original level of distraction? Shouldn't that mean the brain is back in sync with what it has evolved for?" an audience member asked during a lecture I was giving on how our new digital world is making us more easily distracted. It's a brilliant question, and that may well be the case. But there is still a risk that we stand to lose something vital along the way.

Most major cultural, technological and scientific advances were made by people who were able to focus intensely. Coming up with the theory of relativity, discovering the DNA molecule or developing the iPhone—ironically, the optimal tool for distraction—required tremendous focus. Look no further than yourself; regardless of whether you are good at sports, an instrument, programming, writing articles or cooking, you have probably had to push yourself and focus on one thing to become good at it.

"But won't we eventually adapt to our new digital life?" asked the audience member, who wasn't quite convinced by my answer to his question. Indeed, several different technological inventions—such as writing, printing and the clock—influenced not only how people worked and communicated, but probably also how they thought. Our digital lifestyle has the potential to do the same. But that doesn't automatically mean it's all for the better.

The author Nicholas Carr describes how the printing press spread deep focus among large parts of the population. All of a sudden, anyone could open a book and transport themselves into the mind of another person and focus on what they had written down. Carr sees the internet as the opposite of a book. It doesn't facilitate deep thinking but makes us bounce on the surface from one thing to the next, in a perpetual search for the new and for quick dopamine hits. When I first heard Carr's argument, I thought that, sooner or later, we will adapt and become less distracted by screens. But that is not what the evidence suggests. As you read in Chapter 5, we learn more from reading a physical book than a screen. Tests on reading comprehension for screen vs. book have been carried out regularly for more than a decade and the difference between book and screen is *increasing* for every year. The increase is not because we learn more and more from books; it is because we learn less from screens with every passing year. This shows something disturbing: we don't get used to screens—we get more and more distracted by them.

Are we still evolving?

Yes, we are. You and I are not some evolutionary endpoint. Evolution doesn't stop, though it may be slower today. The grim reality is that evolution is a process of weeding out traits that don't provide advantages in a particular environment. Those who have such traits don't survive and don't pass on their genes. Polar bears gradually acquired white fur because those without it ran a greater risk of dying. The reason why Mary with the calorie craving at the beginning of the book had a better chance of passing on her genes was that starvation was common in her world. Those who didn't eat enough didn't survive. Over thousands of years, the craving for calories gradually became more common, as those who lacked it died.

Will we adapt to our new digital world by eventually developing a thumb made for texting or an innate ability to understand programming languages? I don't think so. Evolution is based on traits that are advantageous for our survival or reproduction becoming more common, and those who lack such traits neither surviving nor having children.

Today, we are phenomenal at helping each other survive. The global life expectancy has shot up from 30 years to 73 years in just two centuries. With the help of *in vitro* fertilization, many people can now have children who would otherwise be unable. All this is great, but in a strictly biological sense it means evolution is slowing down. A future where we are born with, say, a natural understanding of programming won't come to fruition because those of us who *aren't* born with it won't die. Thank God, because that most certainly includes me!

Does this mean that humans will never evolve again? Not necessarily. The last few decades have seen tremendous advances in genetic engineering. We have learned how genes affect not only the risks of different diseases, but also our mental characteristics and personality traits. Today we know which genes contribute to everything from body height and hair color to intelligence and how extroverted or neurotic we are. In parallel with this veritable explosion of knowledge, techniques have been developed to modify our genes. These allow us to cut and paste within our genome—almost like moving around text in a Word document! These techniques will most likely be used to modify or remove genes that cause disease, and that is, of course, a good thing. The problem is that the line between disease and characteristic or trait isn't always so clear.

For example, our intelligence depends largely on our genes. But there isn't one single "IQ gene"—instead, hundreds of genes make small contributions to our IQ. You don't need a wild imagination to realize that prospective parents might be tempted to change some of these genes to give their children an IQ that is slightly higher. Today, this is neither permitted nor possible, but in a few years it will be a technical possibility.

In the future, perhaps genetic engineering will be used to alter human traits, from height and personality to athletic ability and intelligence. Many fear that we will hijack our evolutionary development and gradually turn into something else: a new kind of human. If you could step into a time machine and travel a thousand years into the future, who would you meet? Personally, I hope it would be someone who looks and behaves a lot like you and me.

Are we really feeling worse?

In this book, you have read about how more and more people appear to be struggling with mental illness, in parallel with our shift toward an increasingly digital lifestyle. Researchers at Harvard University are now warning that global mental illness is increasing so rapidly that, by 2030, it will result in costs of 16 trillion (16,000 billion) US dollars annually. So far, no country is doing enough to address the problem, even though increased efforts could save 13.5 million lives. "It seems to me that mental health is one of the most neglected areas of human development today," says Harvard professor of global health Vikram Patel.

Mental illness seems to be on the rise in many countries. Among young people, the proportion receiving a psychiatric diagnosis and taking psychotropic medication has more than doubled in ten years.

The figures are so bleak that they risk provoking the very phenomenon they describe. But are we really feeling worse? As it turns out, that question is hard to answer. According to the World Health Organization, no more young people were depressed in Sweden in 2016 than in 1990. Some argue that we are no worse off than before; instead, the increase is due to more people seeking treatment for minor issues and the health services medicalizing normal feelings. So who should we believe? Personally, I belong to the camp that thinks the increase should be taken seriously—though there are undoubtedly those who have unrealistic expectations that psychiatric services will help them with normal emotional slumps that are simply part of life.

When I was in secondary school in the 1990s, contacting psychiatric services was unthinkable—it brought to mind straitjackets and padded walls—so many people struggled without getting help. Today more people are reaching out, which I think is a good thing. It has, for instance, contributed to a 30 percent drop in suicide rates in Sweden since the 1990s.

We aren't happy by nature

As humans, we aren't necessarily happy by nature. In the world that shaped us, half of all people died before their tenth birthday, the average life expectancy was 30 years and people were done in by infections, starvation, murder, accidents and predators, not cancer or cardiovascular disease. In that world, being anxious and vigilant was a survival advantage. It's more likely that your ancestors saw potential disasters left and right—what we today would call anxiety—than that they went around thinking everything was fine, letting their guard down and risking not seeing that snake, lion or neighbor out to kill them. In other words, it's more likely that your ancestors were anxious than that they weren't—remember the smoke detector principle and how feelings guide us toward different behaviors.

We like to speak of an evolutionary pressure to create traits that make organisms more likely to survive in a given environment. Such pressure created white polar bears that are able to camouflage themselves in snowy landscapes, and created cloven hooves that provide the perfect grip on rocks so that the mountain goat can stay balanced on steep alpine hillsides. But never has there been an evolutionary pressure to create a happy *Homo sapiens*—for the simple reason that its odds of survival haven't been very high. "Survival of the fittest" has been as much about avoiding accidents and conflict as it has been about being physically strong, brave and stress resilient. Feelings of anxiety and depression have probably been more important to our survival than joy and calm.

In other words, part of the answer to the question "Why do we feel so bad when we have it so good?" is that nature has never placed a particularly high value on feelings of long-term well-being in humans. Nature has given us feelings of *transient* well-being when we eat yummy food, spend time with friends, have sex or get promoted at work. But these positive feelings tend to be quickly replaced by a desire for even more food and sex, and an even higher position in the workplace. And for good reason: to make sure that we keep going.

There are certain things that make almost everyone feel good:

prioritizing sleep, being physically active, nurturing social relationships and exposing yourself to a healthy amount of stress.

Our ancestors couldn't afford to think *I had a massive meal yesterday, so why bother with food today?* or *My home kept me safe and warm last winter, so I don't have to worry about it almost being winter again.* For 99.9 percent of your ancestors, being in a situation where they had food, safety and shelter for the foreseeable future was extremely rare. Nature hasn't had time to adapt us to the abundance we find ourselves living in, and so we continue to worry, look for dangers and try to satisfy our insatiable need for resources, even though we don't really need to anymore.

Did reading this make you feel discouraged? If so, I can understand. But before you slam the book shut out of sheer desperation, let me say that we aren't necessarily doomed to be unhappy by nature. There are certain things that make almost everyone feel good: prioritizing sleep, being physically active, nurturing social relationships and exposing yourself to a healthy amount of stress. Personally, I think the solution lies in getting more people to *prevent* mental illness—not reflexively assuming that the solution can be found in a pillbox. That psychotropic drugs can do good (because there is no doubt they can—they are life-saving to many) doesn't mean that one in eight adults needs them or that there are no alternatives.

Just because feelings of anxiety and depression have been a natural part of life and have helped us survive doesn't mean we should ignore the suffering they cause. We don't tell people who are short-sighted: "Humans have had bad eyesight throughout history, so just deal with it." We make sure they get glasses. Nor do I think we should say: "People have always felt bad, so just deal with it" Instead, we should try to help those who are unwell by doing something about their condition. The question of whether we are really feeling worse today than 20 years ago is an interesting one, but it shouldn't lead us to ignore the consequences of the predisposition for suffering that nature has encoded in us over millions of years.

The biggest societal change in history

Tabloid headlines like THE INTERNET IS MAKING US STUPID AND DEPRESSED have abounded in recent years, but the issue is far more complex. Digitalization may well be the biggest societal change humanity has ever faced, and all the evidence suggests that we have only seen the beginning. In the coming decades, society will change and become streamlined in ways we can't even dream of. At the same time, digitalization can be compared to another societal change that took place 200 years ago: industrialization. Through the transition to an industrial society, we became better at producing food and fewer people had to go hungry. A French peasant living in the eighteenth century, before industrialization, spent about half of his disposable income on food. Still, that was only enough for 1,800 calories a day—while the recommended daily calorie consumption today is 2,000 for women and 2,500 for men. So even though the French peasants of the eighteenth century spent half of what they earned on food, it wasn't enough to satisfy their hunger.

Fast-forward 300 years and famine has been eradicated in large parts of the world—a development that has saved millions of lives. But if we are a little self-critical, we haven't been very good at managing today's abundance of calories. The consequences of excess weight and obesity top the list of preventable causes of death; today, more people die from overeating than from hunger.

Just as the unrestricted access to calories has brought both advantages and disadvantages for our health, digitalization can be a double-edged sword for our brains. Having all the world's information at your fingertips is a luxury our ancestors could never have dreamed of, even in their wildest imagination. Digitalization can allow us to use our mental faculties even more efficiently, unleashing unimaginable human creativity. But bombarding our brains with thousands of taps and swipes a day has consequences. When distraction becomes the norm, we begin to crave it, even when it doesn't exist.

The more we get used to taking in small pieces of information— text messages, tweets and Facebook likes—the worse we get at taking in big pieces. And in an increasingly complex world, that's a skill we will need.

We must use our digital tools wisely and recognize that there can be downsides to them, otherwise we risk adapting to empty *digital* calories as poorly as we have to the empty calories in the candy aisle. Mobile technology may just as easily turn us into *Homo sapiens 0.5* as *2.0*.

CLOSING WORDS

WE FIND OURSELVES in an alien world, far from the one we evolved in. Despite living in a digital society, we still have a hunter-gatherer brain—busy spotting dangers left and right, easily stressed and distracted and bad at multitasking. In other words, we need an attention fix.

That's why I wrote this book. With more knowledge about the brain and our basic biology, we are better placed to answer questions (some of which might sound initially strange) such as: How come prolonged stress can have devastating consequences for our well-being? How come excessive cell phone use can make us lose interest in the world around us? How do Facebook and Instagram "hack" our reward system by timing when likes are portioned out? How can exercise make us better equipped to cope with stress? Why do we risk ruining our sleep if we keep our phones on our bedside tables? All this can be better understood in light of the brain and the world in which it evolved.

However, it's important to keep one thing in mind. You have probably seen headlines like GET HEALTHY WITH THE CAVEMAN

DIET? or FIND YOUR HAPPY WITH A PALEOLITHIC LIFESTYLE—in other words, headlines claiming that a way of life in better harmony with our origins is more natural, and thus better. But the idea that something is better just because it is natural is a fallacy so common it has its own name: the naturalistic fallacy. Just because our ancestors lived a certain way doesn't mean it was good. They ate the food they could find and that doesn't mean it was healthy—for them or for us.

There are many things that aren't natural. Take contraceptives, for example. The natural result of sex is pregnancy, but today we can prevent that. The natural consequence of severe arrhythmia is death, but today we prevent that with pacemakers. The natural fate of people with poor eyesight is to live out their lives in a constant haze, but today we prevent that with glasses. Simply determining that something is "natural" from an evolutionary perspective makes it neither good nor bad.

We know that physical exercise makes us more focused and stress resilient and improves our memory, because research shows that's how it works. It's not a guess based on the fact that our ancestors moved their bodies more than we do. We know that we become easily distracted by using our phones too much, that we risk ruining our sleep and getting stressed—because research shows just that. It's not a guess based on the fact that our ancestors didn't have cell phones.

An evolutionary perspective helps us understand why we are the way we

are and creates a deeper understanding of the discoveries we make about human nature.

As you will have noticed, this isn't just a book of answers, it's also a book of questions. Questions we need to ask ourselves as we undergo the most rapid behavioral change ever—at a rate that only seems to be accelerating.

Finally, popular science sometimes requires simplification, and this book is no exception. If you want to know more and dig deeper, I have gathered all the studies on which this book is based in the bibliography. I have also compiled a list of tips to help you sleep and feel better, improve your concentration and limit the negative effects of today's digital lifestyle.

ADVICE FOR LIVING IN A DIGITAL AGE

Log your cell phone use. Smartphones are now able to track how much time you spend on them. They will tell you exactly how much of your time your phone is stealing. Awareness is the first step toward change.

Get yourself an alarm clock and a wristwatch. Don't use your phone for functions you don't need it for.

Turn off your phone for an hour or two a day. Let people know that you are taking a couple of hours off from your phone every day to reduce the risk of irritated and angry messages about why you are not responding.

Turn off all push notifications.

Set your phone to black and white. A screen without color triggers less dopamine to be released and this makes a big difference to how long you will want to keep scrolling.

Put your phone on silent when driving. That way, you won't risk being distracted in a critical situation. Receiving a message or a call at precisely the wrong moment can disrupt your concentration when it's needed the most—even if you don't read the message or take the call.

At work

If you are working on something that requires your full attention, don't keep your phone next to you. Put it in another room instead.

Set aside time to check your messages and emails—for example, a few minutes every hour.

When socializing

When you are with friends, keep your phone on silent and not right next to you. Concentrate on the person you are with—that way, you will have more fun together!

Picking up your phone is contagious. If you choose not to, it can create a domino effect where more people follow your lead.

For children and young people

No phones in the classroom! It impairs learning.

Limit screen time and do other things. It's hard to recommend a certain number of minutes of screen time per day, but if you insist on having a figure, two hours is the maximum that adults and young people alike should spend on phones and screens in their free time. Setting aside time for sleeping, eating and getting to work or school, this means spending one-sixth of your waking hours in front of a screen! For children younger than eight, one hour is a reasonable limit. I think it's better to set aside time to do other things, so decide that certain hours should only be used for homework, physical activity or being with friends.

Set a good example. We learn by copying each other. Children do what you do, not what you say.

At bedtime

Switch off your phone and tablet at least an hour before going to bed.

Don't keep your phone in the bedroom if you have the slightest trouble sleeping. Get an alarm clock if you need to be woken up in the morning.

Turn off the ringtone and leave your phone on silent if you need to keep it in the bedroom.

Don't open your work emails just before bed.

Stress

Look out for symptoms of stress (see Chapter 2), but don't forget that they can also be caused by something other than stress. If in doubt, contact your healthcare provider.

Physical activity and the brain

All movement is good for the brain, but getting your heart rate up is ideal. You don't need to run a marathon; from a brain perspective, you will get surprisingly good results just by walking. The best exercise is the exercise you get around to. If you get your pulse up, even better.

If you want to get the most out of physical exercise to reduce your stress levels and improve your concentration, you should make sure to get active three times a week, for 40 minutes each time—preferably getting both sweaty and out of breath.

Social media

Only follow people you actively want to interact with.

Think of social media as a tool for interaction. Actively commenting on other people's posts creates a sense of community and strengthens your connection.

Delete social media apps from your phone and use them only on your computer.

BIBLIOGRAPHY

1. The world that shaped us

Butovskaya, M. et al., "Waist-to-hip ratio, body mass index, age and number of children in seven traditional societies." *Scientific Reports* 7; 1622 (2017): 1–9

Williams, L.E. and Bargh, J.A., "Experiencing physical warmth promotes interpersonal warmth." *Science* 322; 5901 (2008): 606–7

2. Stress, anxiety and depression—evolutionary winners?

Barnes, J. et al., "Genetic contributions of inflammation to depression." *Neuropsychopharmacology* 42; 1 (2017): 81–98

Dhabhar, F.S. et al., "Stress-induced redistribution of immune cells—from barracks to boulevards to battlefields: a tale of three hormones." *Psychoneuroendocrinology* 37; 9 (2012): 1345–68

Jovanovic, H. et al., "Chronic stress is linked to 5-HT(1A) receptor changes and functional disintegration of the limbic networks." *Neuroimage* 55; 3 (2011): 1178–88

Laval, G. et al., "Formulating a historical and demographic model of recent human evolution based on resequencing data from noncoding regions." *PLoS One* 5; 4 (2010): e10284

Raison, C.L. and Miller, A.H., "The evolutionary significance of depression in pathogen host defense (PATHOS-D)." *Molecular Psychiatry* 18; 1 (2013): 15–37

www.socialstyrelsen.se/statistik/statistikdatabas/lakemedel

3. Cell phones—our new drug

Bolton, N., "Steve Jobs was a low-tech parent." *New York Times* (September 10, 2014)

Boumosleh, J.M. and Jaalouk, D., "Depression, anxiety, and smartphone addiction in university students—a cross sectional study." *PLoS One* 12; 8 (2017): e0182239

Bromberg-Martin, E.S. and Hikosaka, O., "Midbrain dopamine neurons signal preference for advance information about upcoming rewards." *Neuron* 63; 1 (2009): 119–26

Krebs, R.M. et al., "Novelty increases the mesolimbic functional connectivity of the substantia nigra/ventral tegmental area (SN/VTA) during reward anticipation: evidence from high-resolution fMRI." *Neuroimage* 58; 2 (2011): 647–55

Meeker, M., "Internet trends 2018." *Kleiner Perkins* (May 30, 2018)

New York Post, "Americans check their phones 80 times a day study." (November 8, 2017)

Retter, E., "Billionaire tech mogul Bill Gates reveals he banned his children from mobile phones until they turned 14." *The Mirror* (April 21, 2017)

Schultz, W. et al., "A neural substrate of prediction and reward." *Science* 275; 5306 (1997): 1593–9, DOI: 10.1126/science.275.5306.1593

Schwab, K., "Nest founder: 'I wake up in cold sweats thinking, what did we bring to the world?'" *Fast Company* (7 July 2017)

Zald, D.H. et al., "Dopamine transmission in the human striatum during monetary reward tasks." *Journal of Neuroscience* 24; 17 (2004): 4105–12

4. Focus—the scarcity of our time

Bowman, L.L. et al., "Can students really multitask? An experimental study on instant messaging while reading." *Computers & Education* 54 (2019): 927–31

Dwyer, R.J. et al., "Smartphone use undermines enjoyment of face-to-face social interactions." *Journal of Experimental Social Psychology* 78 (2018): 233–9

Foerde, K. et al., "Modulation of competing memory systems by distraction." *PNAS* 103; 31 (2006): 11778–83

Henkel, L.A., "Point-and-shoot memories: the influence of taking photos on memory for a museum tour." *Psychological Science* 25; 2 (2014): 396–402

Ito, M. and Kawahara, J-I., "Effect of the presence of a mobile phone during a spatial visual search." *Japanese Psychological Research* 59; 2 (2017): 188–98, DOI: 10.1111/jpr.12143

Mandore, K. et al. "Memory failure predicted by attention lapsing and media multitasking." *Nature* 587 (2020): 87–91

Muller, P.A. and Oppenheimer, D.M., "The pen is mightier than the keyboard: advantages of longhand over laptop note taking." *Psychological Science* 25; 6 (2014): 1159–68

Ophir, E. et al., "Cognitive control in media multitaskers." *PNAS* 206; 37 (2009): 15583–7, DOI: 10.1073/pnas.0903620106

Paul, K., "This is how long it takes to get [sic] regain your concentration after texting on your iPhone." *Marketwatch* (July 31, 2017)

Sparrow, B. et al., "Google effects on memory: cognitive consequences of having information at our fingertips." *Science* 333; 6043 (2011): 776–8

Stothart, C. et al., "The attentional cost of receiving a cell notification." *Journal of Experimental Psychology: Human Perception and Performance* 41; 4 (2015): 893–7

Uncapher, M.R. et al., "Media multitasking and memory: differences in working memory and long-term memory." *Psychonomic Bulletin & Review* 23; 2 (2016): 483–90

Ward, A.F. et al., "Brain drain: the mere presence of one's own smartphone reduces available cognitive capacity." *Journal of the Association for Consumer Research* 2; 2 (2017): 140–54

5. How do screens affect our sleep and mental health?

Alhassan, A.A. et al., "The relationship between addiction to smartphone usage and depression among adults: a cross sectional study." *BMC Psychiatry* 18; 148 (2018)

American Psychological Association, "Stress in America™: Generation Z." Stress in America™ Survey (2018)

Bian, M. and Leung, L., "Linking loneliness, shyness, smartphone addiction symptoms, and patterns of smartphone use to social capital." *Social Science Computer Review* 33; 1 (2015): 61–79

Christensen, M.A. et al., "Direct measurement of smartphone screen-time: relationships with demographics and sleep." *PLoS One* 11; 11 (2016): e0165331

Falbe, J. et al., "Sleep duration, restfulness, and screens in the sleep environment." *Pediatrics* 135; 2 (2015): 367–75, DOI: 10.1542/peds.2014-2306

Hale, L. and Guan, S., "Screen time and sleep among school-aged children and adolescents: a systematic literature review." *Sleep Medicine Reviews* 21 (2015): 50–8, DOI: 10.1016/j.smrv.2014.07.007.

Harwood, J. et al., "Constantly connected: the effects of smart-devices on mental health." *Computers in Human Behavior* 34 (2014): 267–72

Public Health Agency of Sweden, *Nationella folkhälsoenkäten* (National public health survey) (2016)

Sifferlin, A., "Smartphones are really stressing out Americans." *TIME* (February 23, 2017)

Sparks, D., "Are smartphones disrupting your sleep? Mayo Clinic examines the question." *Mayo Clinic News Network* (June 3, 2013)

Thomée, S. et al., "Mobile phone use and stress, sleep disturbances, and symptoms of depression among young adults—a prospective cohort study." *BMC Public Health* 11; 66 (2011)

Warmsley, E.J. et al., "Dreaming of a learning task is associated with enhanced sleep-dependent memory consolidation." *Current Biology* 20; 9 (2010): 850–5

6. Social media—our biggest "influencer"

Appel, H. et al., "The interplay between Facebook use, social comparison, envy, and depression." *Current Opinion in Psychology* 9 (2016): 44–9

Booker, C.L. et al., "Gender differences in the associations between age trends of social media interaction and well-being among 10–15-year-olds in the UK." *BMC Public Health* 18; 321 (2018)

Bosson, J.K. et al., "Interpersonal chemistry through negativity: bonding by sharing negative attitudes about others." *Personal Relationships* 13 (2006): 135–50

Brailovskaia, J. and Margraf J., "Facebook addiction disorder (FAD) among German students—a longitudinal approach." *PLoS One* 12; 12 (2017)

Chang, L. and Tsao, D.Y., "The code for facial identity in the primate brain." *Cell* 169; 6 (2017): 1013–28, DOI.org./10.1016/j.cell.2017.05.011

Diamond, J., *The Third Chimpanzee: The Evolution and Future of the Human Animal* (Harper Perennial, 2006)

Dunbar, R., *Grooming, Gossip and the Evolution of Language* (Faber and Faber, 1996)

Hunt, M.G. et al., "No more FOMO: limiting social media decreases loneliness and depression." *Journal of Social and Clinical Psychology* 37; 10 (2018): 751–68

Konrath, S.H. et al., "Changes in dispositional empathy in American college students over time: a meta-analysis." *Personality and Social Psychology Review* 15; 2 (2011): 180–98

Kross, E. et al., "Facebook use predicts declines in subjective well-being in young adults." *PLoS One* 8; 8 (2013): DOI: org/10.1371/journal.pone.0069841

McAteer, O., "Gen Z is quitting social media in droves because it makes them unhappy, study finds." *PR Week* (March 9, 2018)

McGuire, M.T. and Troisi, A., *Darwinian Psychiatry* (Oxford University Press, 1998)

Meshi, D. et al., "Nucleus accumbens response to gains in reputation for the self relative to gains for others predicts social media use." *Frontiers in Human Neuroscience* 7; 439 (2013)

Nabi, R.L. et al., "Facebook friends with (health) benefits? Exploring social network site use and perceptions of social support, stress, and well-being." *Cyberpsychology, Behavior, and Social Networking* 16; 10 (2013): 721–7

Primack, B.A. et al., "Social media use and perceived social isolation among young adults in the US." *American Journal of Preventive Medicine* 53; 1 (2017): 1–8

Raleigh, M.J. et al., "Social and environmental influences on blood serotonin concentrations in monkeys." *Archives of General Psychiatry* 41; 4 (1984): 405–10

Rizzolatti, G. et al., "Functional organization of inferior area 6 in the macaque monkey. II. Area F5 and the control of distal movements." *Experimental Brain Research* 71; 3 (1988): 491–507, DOI: 10.1007/BF00248742

Shakya, H.B. and Christakis, N.A., "Association of Facebook use with compromised well-being: a longitudinal study." *American Journal of Epidemiology* 185; 3 (2017): 203–11, DOI: 10.1093/aje/kww189

Song, H. et al., "Does Facebook make you lonely? A meta analysis." *Computers in Human Behavior* 36 (2014): 446–52

Tromholt, M., "The Facebook experiment: quitting Facebook leads to higher levels of well-being." *Cyberpsychology, Behavior, and Social Networking* 19; 11 (2016): 661–6

Vosoughi, S. et al., "The spread of true and false news online." *Science* 359; 6380 (2018): 1146–51

Wang, A.B., "Former Facebook VP says social media is destroying society with 'dopamine-driven feedback loops.'" *Washington Post* (December 12, 2017)

Wells, G., "Facebook knows Instagram is toxic for teen girls, its research shows." *Wall Street Journal* (September 15, 2021)

7. What are screens doing to children and young people?

Bloom, H. (2018) "Performance trajectories and performance gaps as achievement effect-size benchmarks for educational interventions." *Journal of Research on Educational Effectiveness* 1(4), 2018: 289–329

Casey, B.J. et al., "The adolescent brain." *Annals of the New York Academy of Sciences* 1124; 1 (2008): 111–26

Chen, Q. and Yan Z., "Does multitasking with mobile phones affect learning? A review." *Computers in Human Behavior* 54 (2016): 34–42

De-Sola Gutiérrez, J. et al., "Cell-phone addiction—a review." *Frontiers in Psychiatry* 7; 175 (2016)

Elhai, J.D. et al., "Problematic smartphone use: a conceptual overview and systematic review of relations with anxiety and depression psychopathology." *Journal of Affective Disorders* 207 (2017): 251–9

Hadar, A. et al., "Answering the missed call: initial exploration of cognitive and electrophysiological changes associated with smartphone use and abuse." *PLoS One* 12; 7 (2017): e0180094

Jiang, Z. and Zhao, X., "Self-control and problematic mobile phone use in Chinese college students: the mediating role of mobile phone use patterns." *BMC Psychiatry* 16; 416 (2016)

Julius, M.S. et al., "Children's ability to learn a motor skill is related to handwriting and reading proficiency." *Learning and Individual Differences* 51 (2016): 265–72

Klass, P., "Let kids play." *New York Times* (August 20, 2018)

Kuznekoff, J.H. and Titsworth, S., "The impact of mobile phone usage on student learning." *Communication Education* 62; 3 (2013): 233–52, DOI.org/10.1080/03634523.2013.767917

Liu, M. et al., "Dose-response association of screen time-based sedentary behavior in children and adolescents and depression: a meta-analysis of observational studies." *British Journal of Sports Medicine* 50; 20 (2016): 1252–8

Lowensohn, J., "Apple's fiscal 2012 in numbers: 125M iPhones, 58,31M iPads." *CNET* (October 25, 2012)

Makin, S. "Searching for digital technology's effects on well-being." *Nature* 563; 7733 (2018): 138–40

Mundell, E.J. "Antidepressant use in US soars by 65 percent in 15 years." *CBS News* (August 16, 2017)

Orben, A. et al., "Windows of developmental sensitivity to social media." *Nature Communications* 13 (2022) (1)2022:1649

Rutledge, R.B. et al., "Risk taking for potential reward decreases across the lifespan." *Current Biology* 26; 12 (2016): 1634–9

Swedish National Board of Health and Welfare, "Kraftig ökning av psykisk ohälsa bland unga" (Steep rise in mental illness among young people) (December 13, 2017)

The World UNPLUGGED. https://theworldunplugged.wordpress.com

TV4. "Färre unga spelar musikinstrument" (Fewer young people play instruments) (December 25, 2017)

Twenge, J.M., "Have smartphones destroyed a generation?" *The Atlantic* (September 15, 2016)

Twenge, J.M. and Campbell, W.K., "Associations between screen time and lower psychological well-being among children and adolescents: evidence from a population-based study." *Preventive Medicine Reports* 12 (2018): 271–83

Wahlstrom, D. et al., "Developmental changes in dopamine neurotransmission in adolescence: behavioral implications and issues in assessment." *Brain and Cognition* 72; 1 (2010): 146–59

Wallace, K., "Half of teens think they're addicted to their smartphones." *CNN* (July 29, 2016)

Walsh, J.J. et al., "Associations between 24 hour movement behaviors and global cognition in US children: a cross-sectional observational study." *The Lancet Child & Adolescent Health* 2; 11 (2018): 783–91

Wilmer, H.H. and Chein, J.M., "Mobile technology habits: patterns of association among device usage, intertemporal preference, impulse control and reward sensitivity." *Psychonomic Bulletin & Review* 23; 5 (2016): 1607–14

8. Exercise—a smart antidote

Althoff, T. et al., "Large-scale physical activity data reveal worldwide activity inequality." *Nature* 547 (2017): 336–9

Aylett, E. et al., "Exercise in the treatment of clinical anxiety in general practice—a systematic review and meta-analysis." *BMC Health Services Research* 18; 559 (2018): DOI.org/10.1186/s12913-018-3313-5 de Greeff, J.W. et al., "Effects of physical activity on executive functions, attention and academic performance in preadolescent children: a meta-analysis." *Journal of Science and Medicine in Sport* 21; 5 (2018): 501–7, DOI: 10.1016/j.jsams.2017.09.595

Ekblom-Bak, E. et al., "Decline in cardiorespiratory fitness in the Swedish working force between 1995 and 2017." *Scandinavian Journal of Medicine Science in Sports* 29; 2 (2019): 232–9

Gomes-Osman, J. et al., "Exercise for cognitive brain health in aging: a systematic review for an evaluation of dose." *Neurology Clinical Practice* 8; 3 (2018): 257–65, DOI: 10.1212/CPJ.0000000000000460

Harris Buchele, H. et al., "Impact of coordinated-bilateral physical activities on attention and concentration in school-aged children." *BioMed Research International* 2018 (2018): 1–7

Marr, B. "How much data do we create every day? The mind-blowing stats everyone should read." *Forbes* (May 21, 2018)

Raustorp, A. and Fröberg, A., "Comparisons of pedometer determined weekday physical activity among Swedish school children and adolescents in 2000 and 2017 showed the highest reductions in adolescents." *Acta Pediatrica* 108; 7 (2019): 1301–10, DOI: 10.1111/apa.1467

Ryan, T.M. and Shaw, C.N., "Gracility of the modern Homo sapiens skeleton is the result of decreased biomechanical loading." *PNAS* 112; 2 (2014): 372–7

Silva, A.P. et al., "Measurement of the effect of physical exercise on the concentration of individuals with ADHD." *PLoS One* 10; 3 (2015): e0122119, DOI:10.1371/journal.pone.0122119

Vanhelst, J. et al., "Physical activity is associated with attention capacity in adolescents." *The Journal of Pediatrics* 168 (2016): 126–31

visualcapitalist.com

9. The future brain—will it adapt?

Carr, N. *The Shallows: What the Internet Is Doing to Our Brains* (W.W. Norton Company, 2011)

Fogel, R. *The Escape from Hunger and Premature Death, 1700–2100* (Cambridge University Press, 2004)

Maguire, E.A. et al., "Navigation-related structural change in the hippocampi of taxi drivers." *PNAS* 97; 8 (2000): 4398–403

Maguire, E.A. et al., "London taxi drivers and bus drivers: a structural MRI and neuropsychological analysis." *Hippocampus* 16; 12 (2006): 1091–101, DOI: 10.1002/hipo.20233

National Centre for Suicide Research and Prevention, the Karolinska Institute

Winerman, L. "Smarter than ever?" *Monitor on Psychology* 44; 3 (2013)

ACKNOWLEDGMENTS

The American cancer physician and author Siddhartha Mukherjee once said that he writes in order to think. I know exactly what he means. Any gap in an argument or a line of thought appears in stark relief when you put it down on paper. However, there is something besides writing that helps me think just as much, and that is discussion with wise people. In no particular order, I would therefore like to express my sincere thanks to the following people who, in various ways, inspired this book: Björn Hansen, Vanja Hansen, Otto Ankarcrona, Mats Thorén, Gustav Söderström, Tahir Jamil, Martin Lorentzon, Minna Tunberger, Daniel Ek, Simon Kyaga, Carl Johan Sundberg, Karl Tobieson, Malou von Sivers, Kristoffer Ahlbom, Jonas Petersson, Anders Berntsson, Viveca Gyberg, Elvira Carlbaum, Jacqueline Levi, Hugo Lagercrantz, Max Tegmark, Olle Palmlöv, Niclas Nyberg, Mattias Olsson, Jock Millgårdh, Malin Sjöstrand, Ted Mannerfelt, Carl Johan Grandinson and Karin Bojs.

Thank you to everyone who has reached out to tell me that you appreciate my writing—at lectures, in the street and in emails and letters. It's hugely inspiring!

As always, a big thank-you to Cecilia Viklund and Anna Paljak at my Swedish publisher Bonnier Fakta, who patiently encouraged and inspired me while acting as a sounding board as I worked on the book.

Gratitude to my US team at Penguin Random House: thank you to my editor, Sarah Curley; production editor Bethany Reis; Christina MacDonald, who Americanized the text; proofreader Mira Park; designers Emma Hall and Erin Yeung; compositor Kim Scott; and operations director and scheduling extraordinaire Meredith Snyder, for bringing the book to the US market.

Thanks also to Nikolas Salmon, who read the English audiobook so well, and to Sofia Heurlin and Hanna Lundkvist at Bonnier Publishing's marketing department, who make sure to spread the word when I have a new book coming out. Thanks also to the competent team at Bonnier Rights for helping my books reach readers in other countries.

Thank you all for being there!

INDEX

transition period 62
and underperformance 53–4
"use it or lose it" approach to
  152–3
see also reward system
broadband, mobile 132
burnout 22, 30

calorie cravings 7–9, 14–15, 157
Campbell, Keith 101–2
candy preference, 7–9, 14–15
Carr, Nicholas 156–7
causality 93
cell phones 37–49
  addiction to 44–9, 73, 106,
    114–16, 133–5, 155
  and anxiety 71
  and appetite 79–80
  attempts to ignore 55–8
  and attention 55–6, 105–6
  bans 123–4, 133, 173
  black-and-white displays 172
  and broadband 132
  and children 47, 113–14, 121–4,
    125–6
  and depression 70, 72–3, 127–31
  distracting nature 55–6
  and dopamine 37–9, 41, 48, 57,
    67–8, 70, 77, 103, 126, 172
  and impulsivity 120–1
  and learning 59–60, 123–4
  logging your use of 171
  losing/giving up 69–70
  loss of control over 133
  and loss of interest in your
    environment 65–8
  and marketing 102–4
  and memory-making 61–3
  and novelty-seeking 41, 48

proliferation 125, 130, 131
  and the reward system 115
  and role-models 172, 173
  and school settings 121–4
  silent mode 55–6, 172, 173
  and sleep 71–2, 77–80, 125–6, 167
  and social media 174
  and stress 70–1
  trimming down the functions
    of 171
  turning off 155, 171
  and uncertainty 42–3, 44
  and young people 113–14, 125,
    127–31
Centers for Disease Control and
  Prevention 127
cerebral cortex 84–5
certainty 42
  see also uncertainty
children 113–35, 173
  addiction to digital technology
    46–7, 114–15
  and body image 93, 95
  development 117–19
  and impulse control 139, 140
  and language skills 124
  and physical exercise 139–43
  and self-esteem 93, 98
  and sleep 78, 79, 124–6
  and social media 97–8, 107
  and stress management 142–3
  see also babies; toddlers
China 73, 128
chlorocebus monkeys 89, 90–2
circadian rhythms 76–7, 125, 140
cognitive bias 145
color 105
compassion 102
competition 92

evolution 6–10, 13, 17–35, 141–2,
    157–9, 161, 168–9
  evolutionary theory of depression
    31–5
  "hacking" 142
  and the reward system 39
  and the stress system 18–21, 39
  and survival 157–8
expectations 41–2
experiences, envy of 94

Facebook 44, 46, 48, 59, 62, 84–9,
    92–6, 102–4, 106–7, 109–11,
    132, 134, 156, 167
  see also Meta
FaceTime 134
facial expressions 135
facts, alternative 109–10
Fadell, Tony 46
fake news 109–10
famine 163–4
fatigue 29
fear
  of missing out 126
  of the unfamiliar 108–10
feelings 33–4
  and the brain 12–13, 15, 21, 31–2
  and decision-making 14–15
  other people's 98–101
  prioritization of negative 15–16
  and survival 12–13
"fight or flight" response 18–20,
    24–5, 29–30, 34, 70, 144
films 100, 129
Five Ants Are More Than Four
    Elephants (TV show) 117
Flynn, James 150–1
Flynn effect 150–1, 153

focus 51–68, 120, 141–2, 156–7, 168
  see also attention; concentration
food supply 163–4
friendships 84–5
frontal lobes 55, 86, 100, 115,
    118–19, 152
future-thought 27–8

gambling 43, 44
gaming 126, 128–9, 134–5, 140–1
Gates, Bill 47
Gazzaniga, Michael 137
genes 158–9
  and depression 32, 33, 35
  mutation 6–8
  passing on 12–13, 31, 39, 68, 157
genetic difference 108
genetic engineering 158–9
genomes 108, 158
Gessner, Conrad 153–4
ghrelin 79–80
girls
  and body image 95
  and mental health issues 127
  and physical inactivity 146
  and screen addiction 133
  and self-esteem 93, 98
  and sleep disturbances 126
  and social media 93, 95, 97–8, 126,
    129–30
glossophobia 24–5
Google 138
"Google effect" 64–5
gossip 81–3
Göteborgsposten 139–40
groups 81–2
  exclusion from 25, 26
  and social status 89

skin color 108
sleep 71–80, 167, 173
  and light exposure 76–8
  requirements 125–6
  and stress 75–7
  and young people 124–6, 127,
    130, 132–3
sleep deprivation 74, 132, 133, 149
sleep disorders 72, 75–6, 80, 124–6,
  129, 155
slot machines 105
smoke detector principle 22–3, 26,
  54, 108, 144, 161
Snapchat 44, 46, 105, 111
sociability 83–8, 107–8, 120
social bonds 82–3
social comparison-making 92–3, 97–8,
  129–30, 132
social exclusion 25, 26
social feedback 88–9, 100, 101
social hierarchy 89–93, 132
social interactions 118–19, 172, 174
social isolation 84, 89, 111
social media 48, 59, 81–111, 126,
  129, 174
  addiction to 46, 106
  and the erosion of empathy 101–2
  giving up on 111
  and life satisfaction 93–5, 111
  and reward centers 44–6
  and well-being in young people
    128, 129
social skills training 118–19
social status 89–93, 102
social withdrawal 30–1, 33, 91, 130
somatosensory cortex 98–9
stage fright 24–5
Stanford University 51–2

starvation 6–8, 12, 15, 31, 107,
  157, 163–4
stomach upsets 19, 29
stress 17–35, 110, 167, 174
  appropriate levels of 22
  and the brain 17, 19–20, 31, 33, 35
  chronic 19–20, 31–2, 34, 91
  and depression 30–1, 34, 72
  and memory 20–1
  and cell phones 70–2, 132
  and negative feelings 16
  and physical exercise 137–8, 142–6,
    168, 174
  sensitivity to 79
  short-term 22
  and sleep 75–7
  and teenagers 126
  warning signs 34
  and young people 126, 130
stress hormones 18, 19
  see also cortisol
stress system 18–22, 25–8, 35,
  70–1, 76
  evolution 18–21, 39
  and hypothetical scenarios 27–8
  and physical exercise 144
striatum 66–7
stroke 74
Stroop test 139
suicidal thoughts 95, 127
suicide rate 160
super-multitaskers 53
survival 7–13, 22–5, 35, 39–40,
  68, 103
  and anxiety 24, 161–3
  and depression 31, 161–3
  and digital addiction 48
  and dopamine 42

survival—*cont.*
  and evolution 157–8
  and feelings 12–13
  and gossip 81–3
  and the HPA axis 18
  and physical exercise 142, 144
"survival of the fittest" 161
sweating 30
Sweden 27, 47, 78, 113–14, 127,
    142, 159–60
Sweden Television 139–40

talking, about ourselves 86–7
technology, adaptation to the human
    106–7
TED talks 59–60
teenagers
  brain energy requirements of 63
  and the dopamine system 116
  and homework 130–1
  impact of screens on 113–35
  and impulse control 115
  and mental health problems
    127–31
  narcissism of 101–2
  and physical exercise 141
  and screen addiction 114–16,
    133, 134
  and screen restrictions 47
  and screen usage times 114, 128
  and sleep 124–6
  and social media 93, 95, 97–8, 129
  and working memory 54–5
  see also adolescence
theory of mind 99, 101, 102
threat perception 16, 18–26,
    31–3, 54, 71, 76, 107,
    144–5, 160–1, 167

TikTok 105
Tinder 138
toddlers 113, 119
TV, children's educational 117
Twenge, Jean 101–2, 130
Twitter/X 93, 105
type A personalities 45
type B personalities 45

uncertainty 41–4, 48
unfamiliar, the, fear of 108–10
United Kingdom 27, 114, 123,
    126–9, 142, 159
United States 114, 127, 128, 133

viruses 33

Wall Street Journal 95
warning signs 34
watches 171
Wikipedia 65, 134
Wired (magazine) 134
work 172
working memory 54–6, 58–9,
    61–2, 135
World Health Organization
    (WHO) 143, 160
writing 118, 122, 123

Yale University 95
young people 173
  and alcohol intake 116
  anxiety in 127–9, 131
  depression in 127–31, 160
  and cell phone addiction 115–16,
    133–4, 135
  and physical inactivity 146
  and risk-taking 116

ABOUT THE AUTHOR

Dr. Anders Hansen is a Swedish psychiatrist, speaker and international bestselling author with his own TV series exploring the human brain. Dr. Hansen's books have sold millions of copies globally and topped bestseller lists around the world. He is the winner of the book of the year Big Health Award 2017 and 2019, and Sweden's Mensa Prize 2018.

Dr. Hansen is also the author of *The ADHD Advantage*, *The Happiness Cure* and *The Mind-Body Method*.